HOSPITALITY
MINISTRY
VOLUNTEER HANDBOOK

HOSPITALITY
MINISTRY

VOLUNTEER HANDBOOK

Equipping You to Serve

First Edition: Year 2019
Prayer Ministry Volunteer Handbook / Outreach, Inc.
Paperback ISBN: 978-1-946453-79-2
eBook ISBN: 978-1-946453-80-8

CHURCHLEADERS
PRESS

Colorado Springs

HOSPITALITY
MINISTRY
VOLUNTEER HANDBOOK

Equipping You to Serve

Written by
Greg Atkinson

General Editor
Mark A. Taylor

CHURCHLEADERS
PRESS

Colorado Springs

CONTENTS

DEDICATION

To my mom, who is my biggest prayer warrior and hero. Your cooking, hosting, and hospitality I witnessed growing up were a constant source of inspiration. Not only did you constantly host family for Thanksgiving and other events, but I remember you having our church staff over to the house for cookouts and swimming. That example was not lost on me. Thank you for setting the bar.

ACKNOWLEDGEMENTS

I'd like to thank Mark A. Taylor, Mary Ann Sibley, Paul Crosby, and Rebecca Carlisle for their constant support, encouragement, and their work on this project. I couldn't have done it without you. Thanks for using your gifts for the Kingdom.

INTRODUCTION

to the *Outreach Ministry Guides* Series

Each of you should use whatever gift you have received to serve others, as
faithful stewards of God's grace in its various forms
(1 Peter 4:10).

*T*his handbook is part of a series designed to equip and empower church volunteers for effective ministry. If you're reading this, chances are you're a church volunteer. Thanks for your willingness to serve!

Several things make this handbook unique:

- The content is specific and practical for your given area of ministry.
- The information is compiled by experienced ministry practitioners—folks who've worked, served, and helped to train others in this particular area.
- It's written with you—a ministry volunteer—in mind.

Within these pages, you'll find three sections. The first gives a brief overview of fundamental principles to provide you with a solid foundation for the ministry area in which you're serving.

Section 2 unpacks various roles and responsibilities. Understanding your role and the roles of your fellow teammates helps the ministry team serve together well.

Finally, Section 3 provides a multitude of practical ministry tools. These ideas and tips will help you demonstrate Jesus' love to the people you serve at your church.

Whether you're a first-time volunteer or a seasoned veteran, my prayer is that the information and practical tools in this handbook will encourage and assist you. May God bless and guide you in your ministry!

— **Matt Lockhart,** Project Manager

INTRODUCTION

to the *Hospitality Ministry Volunteer Handbook*

*E*very good host knows hospitality doesn't happen by accident. The meal won't magically appear. The rooms don't clean themselves. You need a plan and a list of tasks, and hopefully you can share the jobs among several different workers. You need a schedule so everything's ready on time. You know "welcome" means more when it doesn't stop with the mat at the front door.

What's true for hospitable homemakers—and well-run hotels and restaurants—is even more important for local congregations. The hospitality ministry at your church can change the lives of your visitors for eternity. This practical handbook explains why, and then shows you how to plan experiences that show first-time guests what Christian love looks like.

If you're leading a hospitality ministry, discover help here for every aspect of the task, from the parking lot through the end of your worship services. If you're a worker responsible for just one of the many necessary hospitality duties, you'll find yourself in these pages too. Not only will you benefit from a detailed job description of your role, you'll be challenged by examples that describe how your particular responsibility can make a difference.

The last section includes pages and pages of practical tips and ideas. Every hospitality worker is sure to find something new here to make their work more effective.

As you consider the author's advice, you'll catch his enthusiasm for the ministry you've chosen. "The end game is lives transformed by the gospel as they begin a relationship with Christ," he says here.

"The journey of one's spiritual growth may start when that person walks through the doors of our church for the first time."

You have the chance to start many on that most-important journey. This book will help you do so with grace and with excellence.

— **Mark A. Taylor,** General Editor

SECTION 1

HOSPITALITY MATTERS!

*I*t's been said that people will do almost any *what* if they know the *why*. This first section of the book is to explain the why. In these pages you'll see why what you do matters.

CHAPTER 1

THE MINISTRY OF HOSPITALITY

*Y*ou are a vital piece of the puzzle of a thriving church. That's why you have this book.

Consider the invitation to read this book as a coach asking you to get off of the sideline and into the game. The church needs you, and this book will explain just how vital you are to the mission of God and the mission of your local church.

Someone could tell you to stand at a door and greet people when they walk in, but hospitality—true biblical hospitality—is much richer and deeper and more meaningful than standing at a door passing out a bulletin.

It's important to start with the end in mind. Why do we want people to feel comfortable and welcome at our church? A number of reasons deal with biblical themes: loving your neighbor, displaying kindness, gentleness, and compassion. We'll certainly look at these. But first let's consider, what is the end goal?

> *"When your guests return for a second look, you've won 80 percent of the battle of gaining new regular attenders and have drastically increased the chances that they will begin a journey with Christ."* — **Nelson Searcey**

The end game is lives transformed by the gospel as they begin a relationship with Christ and grow in faith year after year.

The journey of one's spiritual growth may start when that person walks through the doors of our church for the first time. You have been given the awesome responsibility to see they're so welcomed and so loved that they will return for a second visit, and a third visit, and eventually assimilated into the body and grow in their faith.

Welcome. That's a word we all long to hear. To know we're welcome, loved, and accepted is a deep desire. Our opportunity as workers in our church's hospitality ministry is to help meet that longing for the many who enter our church doors.

> *"Hospitality means primarily the creation of free space where the stranger can enter and become a friend instead of an enemy. Hospitality is not to change people, but to offer them space where change can take place…. It is not to bring men and women over to our side, but to offer freedom not disturbed by dividing lines."*
> **— Henri Nouwen**

The book *Secrets of a Secret Shopper* describes the challenge that has motivated this handbook.

> *Imagine you're hosting a small group in your home. Imagine you're hosting a birthday party. Imagine you're having friends over for dinner. Can you picture one of these scenarios?*
> *When you have company over, what do you do? You clean house! You prepare. You want to welcome your company with open arms and make sure they feel right at home. This is what this book is about.*
> *Every week thousands of guests visit our local churches. We need to clean house, prepare, and be ready to host them.*

All of us need to have the mindset and expectation that company is coming. How we prepare for and welcome "company" or guests to our churches says a lot about how seriously we take the Great Commission.[1]

You know God dearly loves you. Through the hospitality ministry of your church, you have the chance to share that love with others.

1   Atkinson, Greg. *Secrets of a Secret Shopper*, pg. 22. Rainer Publishing (December 21, 2016)

CHAPTER 2

THE HISTORY OF HOSPITALITY

*W*hat is hospitality? One definition is, "the quality or disposition of receiving and treating guests and strangers in a warm, friendly, generous way." One website describes hospitality this way: "Away from home surrounded by strangers and yet you feel welcome." It goes on to explain that *hospitality* comes from the Latin word *hospes*, meaning both visitor and stranger, and the idea has roots in ancient history.[2]

The word *hospital* has this same Latin word at its root. The word patient comes from *patior*, which is to suffer. Hence, a hospital can be interpreted etymologically as a place where strangers who suffer come to be cared for.

The word *hospice* originated in medieval times, a derivative of this same Latin word. Travel-weary crusaders on their way to the Holy Land found places of refuge in monasteries. Eventually these places of rest came to be called hospices.

Today the "hospitality industry" builds hotels for travelers who need a bed and a meal. But hotels didn't come along in Europe until the eighteenth century. Before that, travelers often relied on the kindness of strangers, and later primitive inns and taverns, for a place to rest.

---

2   https://hospitalityinsights.ehl.edu/the-origins-of-the-hospitality-industry-and-what-lies-ahead

"We don't know where our first impressions come from or precisely what they mean, so we don't always appreciate their fragility." — **Malcolm Gladwell**

But hospitality has an even deeper rich and ancient history. Hospitality is firmly rooted in the Bible and the way of Christ.

In the New Testament, the Greek word translated "hospitality" literally means "love of strangers." Hospitality is a biblical mandate, and we see it both commanded and commended throughout Scripture.

Starting in the Old Testament, we are told to welcome the stranger. Some translations say to welcome the newcomer.

"When a foreigner resides among you in your land, do not mistreat them. The foreigner residing among you must be treated as your native-born. Love them as yourself, for you were foreigners in Egypt. I am the Lord your God" (Leviticus 19:33-34).

Genesis records the story of Abraham showing hospitality to three strangers (Genesis 18:1-15). The book of Hebrews reminds us, "Do not forget to show hospitality to strangers, for by so doing some people have shown hospitality to angels without knowing it" (13:2). And, in fact, this is exactly what Abraham did!

Jesus himself depended on the hospitality of others. "Foxes have dens and birds have nests," he said. "But the Son of Man has no place to lay his head" (Matthew 8:20).

When Jesus was asked what is the greatest of all the commandments, he summed it up by telling us to love God and love your neighbor as yourself (Matthew 22:36-40).

He shows what he means by that in the most amazing story of the Good Samaritan. It's striking to note that loving our neighbor means loving those not like us and has "nothing to do with geography, citizenship, or race. Wherever and whenever people need us, there we can be neighbors and, like Christ, show mercy. This is the essence of hospitality."[3]

Jesus' sobering words should haunt us all: "For I was hungry and you gave me something to eat, I was thirsty and you gave me something to drink, *I was a stranger and you invited me in*, I needed clothes and you clothed me, I was sick and you looked after me, I was in prison and you came to visit me" (Matthew 25:34-36, italics added).

Hospitality is also a specific hallmark for church leaders. In 1 Timothy 3:2 and Titus 1:7-8, Paul lays out important guidelines and criteria for church leadership. He tells the leaders of the church they must be known for being hospitable.

A Biblical Mandate

While hospitality may sometimes be perceived as a unique gifting for some people, Scripture is clear that loving strangers is a biblical mandate to anyone who follows Jesus. Throughout the Old and New Testaments, God specifically commands his people to practice hospitality.

When we welcome the least of these and treat them as valued guests, we welcome Christ himself. And like so much of 1 John shows us, when we love others, we show our love for God.

With the command to practice the loving of strangers so prevalent throughout Scripture, it seems that showing hospitality is one of the primary attributes of individuals—and whole congregations—who follow Jesus. In fact, Jesus says that loving others is the primary way to demonstrate that we're his disciples (John 13:35).

> *For even the Son of Man did not come to be served, but to serve others (Mark 10:45).* **— Jesus**

---

3   https://www.gotquestions.org/Bible-hospitality.html

Perhaps one of the most grace-filled examples of hospitality in the Old Testament is the system that God sets up allowing all people, both rich and poor, to approach the tabernacle and offer sacrifices to him for their forgiveness. Via this system, travelers could come to the temple to offer sacrifices and worship God. No one's economic status excluded them.

In the same way, because of Jesus' sacrifice on the cross for our sins, we are able and welcome to come to him. Everyone—including those who don't yet know God—should be able and welcome to come to his Church, which Paul calls "God's household" (1 Timothy 3:15).

When we welcome strangers into our church and show love to them, we emulate his love and compassion—the same hospitality he showed us as he welcomed us, not as "foreigners and strangers," but as "members of his household" (Ephesians 2:19-20). A church that welcomes strangers and practices true hospitality is a community where God dwells.

Are you a part of a church that loves strangers? Would your surrounding community say you are a church of love and compassion where anyone would feel welcome?

Do the hearts and attitudes—not just actions—of your people reflect a true desire to bring others into God's household? Do you see how your congregation's hospitality can lead strangers to feel the love of God and experience transformation that will affect their eternity?

A few verses from Ephesians are especially challenging: "As you read over what I have written to you, you'll be able to see for yourselves into the mystery of Christ. None of our ancestors understood this. Only in our time has it been made clear by God's Spirit through his holy apostles and prophets of this new order. The mystery is that people who have never heard of God and those who have heard of him all their lives (what I've been calling outsiders and insiders) stand on the same ground before God. They get the same offer, same help, same promises in Christ Jesus. The Message is accessible and welcoming to everyone, across the board" (Ephesians 3:4-6 MSG).

"Perhaps because it's so rare in our times, welcome beautifully expresses God's vision for human relationships. In a culture that emphasizes fast meals, online friendships, and casual hook-ups, *hospitality is a truly countercultural experience.*

Showering tangible love on those we know—and on those we don't—allows people to experience the love of Jesus in ways they don't see coming.

Hospitality is good faith in action."[4]

---

4   https://annvoskamp.com/2016/03/1-remarkably-simple-way-to-live-good-faith-when-society-thinks-people-of-faith-are-irrelevant-extreme

CHAPTER 3

YOUR MISSION AND THE IMPORTANCE
OF FIRST IMPRESSIONS

Mission and Calling

The apostle Paul compares the church to a human body (1 Corinthians 12:27), and he says the work of the pastor is to equip those various parts of the body "for works of service" (Ephesians 4:11-12). Those works can include the many different roles in your hospitality ministry: parking team, greeters, ushers, welcome center hosts, section hosts, and more. Obviously, no pastor can fill all those roles. But you can help make your church body healthy and effective as you claim a ministry that best fits the gifts God has given you.

> *Each of you should use whatever gift you have received to serve others, as faithful stewards of God's grace in its various forms (1 Peter 4:10).*

Moses had to learn to delegate (Exodus 18:13-26) and thus extend his ability to serve. Likewise, even Jesus multiplied himself through his apostles (Mark 3:13-15). He chose, taught, and empowered them to do his work on earth.

You've been chosen too. You've been given this handbook because you can play a crucial role in your congregation's mission of becoming a safe and welcoming place for all who enter in.

First Impressions

"My pleasure." Those are the two famous words heard from every Chick-fil-A employee across the US when you say, "Thank you."

The phrase is important because it communicates a desire to serve another person. The phrase is remembered because it is the same at every location across America. The phrase is impactful, because it is a breath of fresh air in today's hurried world and stands in stark contrast to the response and attitudes you may experience from many who are hired to serve you.

Chick-fil-A's goal is to treat every guest "with honor, dignity, and respect." The company is committed, through key actions they call Second-Mile Service, to create remarkable experiences for guests.[5] Have you thought about creating remarkable experiences for guests at your church?

Disney has long been the benchmark for customer service and hospitality. Disneyland is known around the world as the "happiest place on earth," largely because guests know they will be treated as VIPs with over-the-top customer service. This was envisioned, modeled, and encouraged by Walt Disney himself—decades later, it remains the gold standard of how to treat others well.

The following quote is widely attributed to Walt Disney: "Whatever you do, do it well. Do it so well that when people see you do it, they will want to come back and see you do it again, and they will want to bring others and show them how well you do what you do."

Imagine your hospitality ministry serving people so well they want to come back to your church. In fact, they want to bring others and show them how well you honor and treat your guests. What a wonderful goal for volunteers in this ministry.

---

5   *It's My Pleasure* (book by Dee Ann Turner) – pg. 117, 118. Elevate; Gld edition (November 3, 2015)

Here's what Tom Peters and Bob Waterman had to say on the subject of service in their groundbreaking book, *In Search of Excellence*: "Whether or not they are as fanatic in their service obsession as Frito, IBM, or Disney, the excellent companies all seem to have very powerful service themes that pervade the institutions. In fact, one of our most significant conclusions about the excellent companies is that, whether their basic business is metal-bending, high technology, or hamburgers, they have all defined themselves as service businesses."[6]

And no institution should be more committed to service than the church! We're much more than a business, but we'd still do well to think of our activities as in the service business. When Jesus wanted to show his disciples the true meaning of leadership, he wrapped a towel around his waist, got on his hands and knees, and began to wash their feet. Jesus modeled serving and servant leadership.

Horst Schultze, formerly of the Ritz Carlton Hotel Group, was known for motivating and guiding his employees by reminding them daily that they were "Ladies and gentlemen serving ladies and gentlemen." It was Ritz Carlton that first responded with, "My pleasure," and it's where Truett Cathy got the idea.

Why It Matters

Chick-fil-A, Disney, Ritz Carlton, and a long list of other companies excel at customer service. Why does this matter to those of us who serve in the local church?

First, if a fast food restaurant, hotel, or theme park gets the importance of hospitality and making guests feel welcome, how much more should the local church?

---

6   Franks, Danny. *People Are the Mission* (pp. 59-60). Zondervan. Kindle Edition. Copyright 2018.

Chick-fil-A is a Christian-owned company built on Christian values of hospitality. Their standard of Second-Mile Service refers to Jesus' Sermon on the Mount where he says, "If anyone forces you to go one mile, go with them two miles" (Matthew 5:41).

Second, we want to instill and live out a culture that oozes hospitality. How can our churches ooze hospitality? Well, it takes a relentless pursuit of the vision of excellence that culminates in an exceptional experience for both members and guests. This happens when we make values like generosity, hospitality, grace, compassion, and excellence habits rather than rare moments.

As Bob Goff's bestselling book title reminds us: *Love Does*. Love is a verb. We must put feet and action behind our talk about and commitment to the love of Jesus. This means we are the hands and feet of Christ to a broken, hurting, and lost world. What does that look like and how can we live this out?

Jesus spelled it out in two sentences most Christians have heard quoted many times. He said to go and make disciples (often called the Great Commission, Matthew 28:19-20) and love your neighbor as yourself (often called the Great Commandment, Matthew 22:39). Go and tell people and be sure to love people. It's always about people. As Danny Franks says, "People are the mission."

Preacher and Professor Haddon W. Robinson said, "We don't teach the Bible; we teach people the Bible."[7]

Truett Cathy, Founder of Chick-fil-A, often said, "We are not in the chicken business. We are in the people business."[8]

Ministry—your ministry—is about people. Your hospitality team will influence the culture for your whole church. People first.

---

7   https://blog.logos.com/2019/01/haddon-robinson-on-the-2-essential-elements-of-preaching

8   ttps://books.google.com/books?id=xpLeDQAAQBAJ&pg=PT14&lpg=PT14&dq=Truett+Cathy,+Founder+of+Chick-fil-a

As pastor Perry Noble has said for years, "Every number has a name, every name has a story, and every story matters to God."[9]

As Christ followers, we are called to live on mission. This means being a good coworker, a good friend, and a good neighbor. Jesus' call to love our neighbor still applies today, and when you gather to worship together on a weekend, someone's neighbor may walk through the doors of your church—it could even be your literal neighbor. How they are received and how they leave feeling determine whether or not they will return.

When guests visit your congregation, they are filled with all sorts of emotions. Some of the strongest emotions they may feel are fear, anxiety, and skepticism. They are looking for an excuse to leave or never return. Something that may seem small to you— you and another greeter are so busy in your own conversation that you don't even notice this person coming to the door— could cause the newcomer to turn around and head back to the car.

Andy Stanley writes, "We must remove every possible obstacle from the path of the disinterested, suspicious, here-against-my-will, would rather-be-somewhere-else, unchurched guests. The parking lot, hallways, auditorium, and stage must be obstacle-free zones."[10]

The point is well taken that we have an amazing opportunity to create an environment that is warm and welcoming.

"Hospitality is not to change people, but to offer them space where change can take place." **— Henry Nouwen**

---

9   https://perrynoble.com/blog/every-number-has-a-name

10   Stanley, Andy. *Deep & Wide: Creating Churches Unchurched People Love to Attend*, pg. 210. Zondervan; Expanded edition (February 9, 2016)

Words of Life

We're starting off this book with tremendous examples of hospitality and yes, even customer service. Why? Because what we, the church, have to offer is so much more than chicken nuggets and roller coasters. We are able to share words of life to those who desperately need to hear them.

What we do when we gather every weekend matters. It has eternal weight and impact. Your pastor, more than likely, has spent the majority of the week preparing a sermon to share the good news of the gospel. But, in reality, the sermon starts in the parking lot.

We need to *be* the gospel, not just proclaim it with words. We need to live out the gospel and demonstrate our faith by putting it into action as the book of James teaches us.

When someone walks through the doors of our church, they are making a huge spiritual decision, whether they realize it or not. God is already at work in their heart, whether they realize it or not.

And their walking up to your church is probably the answer to someone's prayers. A parent, child, spouse, or friend has been begging God for this guest to come or return to church, and today is the day that prayer is answered.

When the Prodigal Son returns (Luke 15), the Bible says the Father runs to welcome his son home, hugging him and kissing him, restoring him. In all three of the parables in Luke 15 (the lost sheep, the lost coin, and the lost son), there was great rejoicing when the one that was lost was found.

When is the last time you visited a church? When is the last time *you* were the guest? When is the last time you walked into unfamiliar territory and felt lost and outnumbered?

In his book *Jim and Casper Go to Church*, Jim Henderson encourages every pastor to send church members for anonymous visits to other congregations. Such visits would give you and other members of your hospitality team much insight into how to welcome visitors.

Henderson's challenge is pointed: "Unless we're willing to remove the handles from the front doors of our churches and publicly say to outsiders, 'We don't care what you think,' the church must become more reflective and repentant about how outsiders perceive us." [11]

How Do We Look?

When you invite an unchurched friend to visit your congregation, you'll see in a new way how your congregation looks to outsiders. You want everything to be perfect for your guest.

The Entrance. You bite your nails as you wait in the lobby to greet your friend and guest. You hope the parking lot attendants are smiling, waving, and pointing your friend to first-time guest parking. You hope your friend is greeted warmly as she and her child walk up.

You pray that the check-in procedure for your first-time guest is smooth and efficient. You hope your guest's child is greeted by comforting, welcoming faces, giving your friend the confidence needed to drop off her child in a foreign environment with strangers. You hope the children's ministry rooms are clean, safe, and secure.

When you walk your guest to the Information Center, you pray she will encounter someone who knows and does the job well. You think, *This is my friend for whom I've been praying for three years. Can you make her want to come back? Can you help her see Jesus through your actions and words?*

The guy at the Information Center does his job. Your guest receives a welcome packet, which includes a note from the senior

---

11   Henderson, Jim. Jim and Casper *Go to Church: Frank Conversation about Faith, Churches, and Well-Meaning Christians* (pp. 147-148, 149-150). Tyndale House Publishers, Inc.. Kindle Edition. Tyndale Momentum (March 1, 2012)

pastor and info on the vision and values of the church. Then she is pointed toward the worship auditorium.

The Service. Together, you and your invitee walk into the auditorium and determine where to sit. The back isn't an option because it's difficult to see the front, and you don't want your guest to feel disconnected.

You hope someone will come introduce himself or herself and welcome your friend. Why? Because friendliness puts people at ease. It helps them feel welcomed and safe.

So, you sit with your friend and make small talk, all the while trying not to worry. Then it hits you: *The sermon! What if the pastor talks on sin? What if he preaches on Hell?* And then you almost have a heart attack. *What if he preaches on money?*

You get the picture. Pastors encourage the congregation to invite their friends, family, neighbors, coworkers, and classmates, and when they do, we must steward it well. All across the world, every Sunday is someone's first Sunday. For you, this week someone may walk through the doors of your church for the first time ever. And that, my friend, is a big deal.

CHAPTER 4

BEST PRACTICES

*S*how love. Author Gary Chapman wrote an international bestselling book titled *The 5 Love Languages*. According to Chapman, there are five love languages: Words of Affirmation, Acts of Service, Receiving Gifts, Quality Time, and Physical Touch.

Seth Switzer, in the Weekend Worship and Guest Services Facebook Group, suggests how to speak all five of these languages as we show love to our guests:

1. Words of Affirmation: "It's good to see you today." "I love that coat." "We're honored that you're here."
2. Acts of Service: Holding the door, giving out coffee, or directing someone to a parking spot.
3. Receiving Gifts: Giving a mug, pen, gift card, or T-shirt.
4. Quality Time: Taking a moment to say hi, avoiding long conversations with other hosts or regular members.
5. Physical Touch: A high five, handshake, or fist bump.

"Individual commitment to a group effort, that's what makes a team work, a company work, a society work, a civilization work." — **Vince Lombardi**

Smile (it's your greatest weapon) and make eye contact. These are the two simplest and easiest wins for you and your team.

Stay positive. Some people can bring down the whole mood of a room with one negative comment or interaction. Don't be that person.

29

Be prompt. Remember the adage, "early is on time and on time is late." Nothing can pull down team morale like the same person being late every week.

Follow the program. There is no room for renegades and rebels. If your church wears nametags, lanyards, or T-shirts, you need to wear them as well. There's no room for people who buck the system or think they are too cool. Pay attention to your church's unspoken or spoken dress code. If all the ushers are wearing T-shirts, don't be the guy that shows up in a three-piece suit. Practice conformity and uniformity.

Stay positive. Be polite, courteous, respectful, and accountable. Show up with a great attitude. Be cheerful and agreeable.

Find your replacement. Doing so gives you rock star status! If you're going to miss, don't just drop your absence in your team leader's lap. Tell him or her you'll be gone and who will fill your spot.

Demonstrate compassion and generosity. They go hand-in-hand with hospitality.

Commit to excellence. Remember, excellence honors God.

"Excellence is an art won by training and habituation."
— Aristotle

Own the mission of the church. Be a carrier of the vision.

Focus on people. Hospitality ministry is highly relational, not transactional (simply passing out bulletins). We are there to serve and fellowship with real people, not simply perform a function like a robot.

You are not a part of a monumental team like hospitality simply to pass out bulletins. If you can be replaced with a table, you're not doing it right.

Stay teachable and coachable. Display a quiet confidence, mixed with genuine humility. You don't know it all. What others have said is true for you: the more you learn, the more you realize how much you don't know.

When your leader schedules a training session, be open to feedback. Your presence and teachable attitude say more about your relationship with God and others than you may think.

> *"What happens "backstage" will end up "on-stage." If we aren't friendly with each other... smiling and saying "good morning" and things like that, then we'll have a similar attitude toward our guests."*
>
> **— Van Arsdale France**

Work toward self-awareness. Ask yourself, "How do I come across to others? Am I being loud? Rude? Insensitive? Rebellious? Negative? Backward? Aloof?"

Be a servant. Are you a giver or a taker?

"When the original Disneyland in Anaheim opened in 1957, Walt Disney was walking around the park with his executive leadership team. Walt noticed one executive stepping over a piece of litter and asked him, 'Why didn't you pick that up?' The man replied, 'It's not my job to pick up litter.' He didn't last the day.

This may seem draconian, but today even the park general managers walk around picking up litter."[12]

Your over-the-top service may include changing a tire, changing a diaper, sweeping up trash, cleaning up vomit, shoveling snow, or escorting people in the rain with umbrellas. Do whatever it takes to make your guests feel at home and welcome.

---

12   https://www.linkedin.com/pulse/5-disney-customer-service-secrets-everyone-should-know-daniel-davey

Look for the "milkshake moments." Be ready to meet needs you've never before encountered in ways that may be outside the ordinary. *Milkshake Moments* is the title of a book by Steven S. Little, and he explains this concept perfectly.

At the end of a long day Little retreated to his hotel room and called room service to ask for a vanilla milkshake. The friendly voice on the other end of the line informed him that the hotel does not serve milkshakes. So Little tried again.

"Do you have vanilla ice cream? Do you have milk?" When the answer to both was yes, he placed his order. Soon a waiter knocked on his door and brought in the bowl of ice cream, the half glass of milk, and the long spoon Little had requested. The hotel had everything he needed for his vanilla milkshake. But the hotel employee wasn't creative or thoughtful or assertive enough to create one.[13]

We can do better than that room service waiter.

Think "whatever, whenever." Those words are the motto of the W hotel group to describe a culture that can characterize our hospitality ministry. Guests at the chain used to be frustrated by the number of calls they had to make to get something done. Sometimes they were sent to two or three different departments before their need was met.

Now, W guests simply push the "Whatever, Whenever" button, and their request is handled with one call.

We can learn from this example. Instead of saying "I don't know" or telling a guest to take their request to someone else, we can do our best to meet their need, whatever it may be.

Be a team player. If a leader asks you to do something, go somewhere, wear something, or say something (within reason and not contrary to Scripture), do it. Be agreeable.

---

13   Little, Steven. *The Milkshake Moment*, pp. 6–7. Wiley, copyright 2008

Let leaders lead. Know when to talk and when to stay silent, especially at meetings conducted by your team leader or pastor.

Pastors and leaders don't need people telling them how to do their job. They need you to perform to the best of your ability without picking up any sense of arrogance, ego, bossiness, rebellion, or troublemaking.

Attend meetings. You may have heard "Culture eats strategy for lunch every day of the week." It's important that you as a team member are on the same page with your team leader and the rest of your team.

This is why so many churches across the world have team huddles before their services (see Chapter 12). Team huddles are a way to reflect, pray, inspire, celebrate, cast vision, and get focused for your day of serving

Know your campus layout.

Protect your pastor. Don't bother the pastor with unimportant things. Unless there's a true emergency, wait until after the service; even better, hold your question or issue until Monday.

"Every person that fills a seat has a soul." — **Paul Crosby**

Stay sensitive to the Spirit. Discern what God is doing in the moment. Not everyone is on the same spiritual level. And those who didn't grow up in the church may surprise you with their reactions or questions. A negative word or look from you could even cause them to question coming to your church.

Avoid insider language. Don't tell people to go to the narthex. They don't know what that is. Don't use words like "Zebra" and "Kangaroo" when directing guests with kids to their classrooms. Say "nursery" or "elementary," or better yet, walk them there yourself and explain what they need to know.

Give instructions with humility, gentleness, and patience. There's a right way and a wrong way to ask guests to move in their seats or wait in the lobby. The following two Scripture passages provide us with great guidance:

"Let your gentleness be evident to all. The Lord is near" (Philippians 4:5).

"The fruit of the Spirit is love, joy, peace, forbearance, kindness, goodness, faithfulness, gentleness, and self-control" (Galatians 5:22-23).

Stay at your post the entire service. Great volunteers bookend the experience. Be present before, during, and after the service. Greeters, ushers, parking lot attendees, and welcome desk hosts don't just say "hello." They say "goodbye."

Be proactive. If you see a potential problem or area of concern, address it. Even better, though, try to head something off so it doesn't become a problem. Being proactive is being preemptive and preventive.

When you notice someone down, frustrated, hurt or just not themselves, take the initiative to ask if they need someone to talk to or ask how you can pray for them. Take the time to listen and serve. Be the hands and feet of Christ to those you come in contact with; it's what we're called to do.

See interruptions as opportunities. When someone troubles you with a request or a question, take it seriously and pay attention to what God may be doing in that moment. Make sure not to stay so focused on a task that you miss the power of the moment.

"All Christians are called to be hospitable. But it is more than serving a meal or filling a bed, opening our door—it is to open ourselves, our hearts to the needs of others. Hospitality is not just shelter but the quality of welcome behind it." — **Dorothy Day**

Remember, there is no "off-week." Even on weekends when you're not on duty, you can be friendly and inviting. Greet others, and especially seek out new faces. Take a few extra minutes in the lobby and look for newcomers you can engage in conversation.

Be friendly without being too friendly. Nobody wants to be creeped out.

Be aware of your body language. You may have heard the often-quoted—and often-misused—rule that communication is only 7 percent verbal and 93 percent nonverbal. The nonverbal component was made up of body language (55 percent) and tone of voice (38 percent). Whether or not those numbers are exact, the concept holds true—body language is vitally important to be aware of.

Eye rolling and/or lack of eye contact is a killer to a guest. In their book *The Come Back Effect*, authors Jason Young and Jonathan Malm write:

> *There's natural body language we all display in different circumstances.*
> *When we feel threatened, we cross our arms to feel protected, we avoid eye contact, we frown. ... When we're glad to be around someone, we smile, we brighten our eyes, we open our arms in welcoming gestures, we make eye contact. ...*
> *Those positive body language elements are all signs to the guest that we are listening and happy to be doing it. And while a guest might not be fully aware of it, their subconscious is taking cues from our body language and informing them whether they're in a safe environment.[14]*

---

14   Young, Jason. *The Come Back Effect: How Hospitality Can Compel Your Church's Guests to Return* (pp. 75-76). Baker Publishing Group. Kindle Edition. Copyright 2018

Remember to smile. Smiling is a universal sign that someone is happy and at peace. Smiling is also contagious. The more smiles you give, the more you receive.

It's also very important to stay hands-free when you serve. Our guests should never have to compete for attention with our electronics or our beverage. Put away your cell phone. If you want coffee, arrive extra early and drink it before you go to your post.

Over communicate to your team leader. If you ran out of some supplies or noticed a problem, talk to your team leader or pastor after the service, or send them an email when you get home.

Keep your leaders up-to-date on what happened over the weekend and how you can improve as a team. Take ideas to your ministry director, but don't be offended if they don't implement them.

Focus on those with special challenges, needs, or disabilities. We are at our best when we serve those who are the weakest.

Work for unity. Maintain a positive team spirit and don't be argumentative. Seek peace among everyone on your team.

Try to reproduce yourself. Look for others not serving who could step into your position. The best thing anyone can do is work themselves out of a job.

As a team member, you are your church's best recruiter to build the hospitality team. Think about whether your team looks like the makeup of the community where your church is located. Multigenerational and multiethnic teams are a beautiful thing to behold and a sign of a thriving and healthy church. Don't be afraid to let teenagers serve alongside you.

CHAPTER 5

HOSPITALITY MINISTRIES ARE FOR EVERY CHURCH

*T*he lists of roles and positions described in this handbook may seem daunting to the small church leader. It would be natural for him or her to ask, "Where do I start?"

We've found it's best to show a large-scale hospitality ministry (to allow you to see where it can grow to), realizing that many will scale it back and start with Version One. That's great!

As we stated earlier in the book, parking teams are not just for directing traffic. We think it is best practice to have a presence in your parking lot, regardless of church size. If people don't need any help finding a parking space, you are still the first impression of your church and can hold a greeting sign and smile and wave.

For many churches, ushers and greeters will be a combined role. Oftentimes in a small church, a door greeter will pass out bulletins and also be ready, willing, and able to assist if help is needed when it comes to seating guests. Look at the job descriptions for these roles and combine them as you can.

The section host concept is a huge plus for the small church. The need for this key role of your hospitality ministry is well documented in Thom Rainer's book *Becoming a Welcoming Church*. His research shows that many guests will not return to a church if they are ignored while they're sitting in the auditorium. They appreciated being greeted in the parking lot and at the door, but since no one talked with them when they sat down before service, they would not return.

You can get lost in a large church. This is not the case in a smaller church. If you sit down in a room of 50 to 80 people and no one notices you or stops by to say hello, this is a painful experience. Adding section hosts (even if it's one person in the front of the auditorium and one person in the back of the auditorium) will help your guests feel right at home.

Karl Vaters is a small church pastor. He blogs for *Christianity Today* on leading a small church. When Karl spoke at the First Impressions Conference in September of 2018, he said that first impressions are important in any congregation, but they are essential for the small church.

Vaters said, "You can't afford not to be nice and friendly when you're in a small church. Everyone knows who is new. You have to make sure to help them feel welcome."

This book is about the biblical mandate and practice of hospitality. Whether you're a church of 50 people or a church of 5,000 people, guests need to know you care about them and are glad they showed up.

Our encouragement to the small church (which is the majority of congregations in North America) is to start somewhere. Maybe station one person outside to wave at people as they pull onto your property. Maybe have someone open the front door and someone inside passing out bulletins and saying, "Good morning."

In time your congregation will grow, and so will your team. But you must start somewhere. If your church is not friendly with 10 people, it won't be friendly with 1,000. Every church, including the smallest churches, needs a hospitality ministry. [15]

---

15 The author of this handbook, Greg Atkinson, works with churches of all sizes and worships at a church plant of 50 people. Greg wrote this book, with help from his pastor, and with his small home church in mind.

SECTION 2

THE "WHO" OF HOSPITALITY MINISTRY

*T*his section unpacks a variety of roles within a church's hospitality ministry team. Having a good understanding of your role, as well as the roles of your fellow team members, will help the team work together well. Included in Chapters 7-11 are a variety of case studies that can be reviewed and discussed.

CHAPTER 6

MEET OUR GUESTS

*W*ho visits your church? Are the first-timers all alike? "Of course not," you may say. But only after you have the chance to meet a few of them will you see the wide variety of experiences and reasons for attending among those who attend your church for the first time. Here are a few of the visitors your church might welcome this week.

People Like These

Luis is in his mid-thirties and never married. It has been a few years since he last attended church. His parents always took him to church as a kid. But life has been really busy, and he does love to travel. Luis has come to realize, though, that all his work and travel has disconnected him from meaningful relationships. And with his recent move away from family, Luis thought church might be a place to get connected.

Monique is a single mom of two children, ages 7 and 9. She has been struggling alone with her kids for more than five years, and a neighbor has been inviting her to church for more than a year. Monique has always declined because, first, life is just too busy for a single mom to add one more thing to the calendar. And second, church people have always seemed judgmental, and that's the last thing Monique needs in her life. But she decided she would give church a try just this one time. Then she can tell her neighbor she came, and that will be the end of the invitations.

Jim and Nancy have been married for three years, and they look like they just walked out of the "Coolest Couples" magazine. But they have been unable to get pregnant and don't know how to deal with the disappointments and failures. The stress of it all is threatening their marriage. They haven't really tried church. Yes, they have attended Easter and Christmas, because that's what you do on holidays. Their friends say a lot of good things about this church and the "God-thing" they need. Why not give it a try? They think it will be interesting to see church not at its holiday best.

Rachel, a single woman in in her late twenties, lives just a block from the church building and has been driving by for more than a year. But today she decided to turn in to the parking lot. Even after being intimidated with all the cars and size of the church, something said, just try it.

In the next few chapters, watch as these guests come to your church for weekend worship. And, in the process, we'll look at the members of the hospitality ministry who make them feel welcome.

CHAPTER 7

HOSPITALITY STARTS
IN THE PARKING LOT

A CASE STUDY

IT'S ALREADY BEEN a whole day's work for **Monique**. She has been fighting the "what-to-wear" war with her kids, and then it hit her: "What will I wear? I don't have a fancy outfit for church!" But the kids are already dressed, so she throws on whatever is clean and heads out the door.

As Monique approaches the parking lot entrance, she wonders if this was a mistake. She really needs to get the laundry done before another workweek and whispers, "I hope this doesn't take all morning."

As she gets ready to turn in, she sees a man in a bright orange vest, smiling and waving at her like he knows her, but he doesn't. *Okay*, she thinks to herself. *This might not be too bad.*

Then she notices a large sign: "Front Row Parking for First-Time Guests. Just flash your lights!"

"Wow!" she says out loud and hits the button to flash her lights.

Just then a woman named Vicky, in the same bright orange vest, is waving at her to come her way. As Monique pulls closer and slows down, Vicky leans in. "Hey! Good morning!" she says. "We are so glad you are here today. I see your lights flashing, and we have the best parking spot for you. See that volunteer ahead waving at us? He will guide you. Thank you for visiting us today!"

Monique thinks, *Who are these people?! This is not at all what I've heard about "church people." I guess all I need to do now is park. Whew!*

> **Hospitality volunteer:** How would you behave or react in a situation like this? Discuss this question with others on the Hospitality Ministry Team.

The Parking Lot Attendant

*T*hese volunteers provide the first human contact newcomers will experience at your church. The first face of the church is here! The attitude and body language of these team members will set the tone for the rest of the visitor's experience.

At first, some will say this position is unnecessary. "People know where to park. We don't need anyone out there."

That may or may not be true. And even if your parking lot is super simple or has dozens of open spaces, actual parking is *not* the primary reason to have volunteers in the parking lot.

It's true you don't see people helping you park at the grocery store or the mall. But if the local church is to be one safe place for people to find uncommon comfort, radical refuge, unimaginable peace, unspeakable joy, and a God who is exactly who he says he is, then church should and must show people something more and better than anything the world can offer.

This role is, first, to **create that welcoming environment** with joy and intention. Think of the doorman at a fancy hotel. Of course, people know how to open a door. But the doorman's job is to greet and tell guests to have a great day. His smile may be the only one someone sees all day.

A smiling parking lot attendant sends the message that the guest made the right choice to come to your church that day.

This is as important when your parking lot is empty as when it's full. Have you ever pulled into a restaurant parking lot that was empty? Maybe it's closed. Maybe the regulars know to park in the back. Maybe it's just a bad restaurant.

An empty church parking lot on a Sunday could send several messages to a first-time visitor:

- *I came too early.* Many first-time guests arrive 20 or even 30 minutes early to make sure they can find the church, get settled, and quiet their nerves.
- *I'm at the wrong place.* The smiling parking lot attendant confirms that the church is expecting people to be there at that time.

There are too many (preventable) stories of people turning around and leaving after driving into a lonely church parking lot. We pray and ask for God to bring people to us, so why are we not anticipating that God will answer our prayers? Why aren't we ready to welcome them as their tires meet our pavement?

The local church should be the one place on planet earth where anyone can know they will be 100 percent welcomed and wanted and seen. And it starts in the parking lot.

Remember that vision when seeking parking lot volunteers. You're seeking friendly, welcoming volunteers for the parking lot, not robots just pointing and directing.

Second, the role is to **safely direct people to the most convenient parking spots**. This raises several questions:

· How do we serve first-time visitors?

Having clearly marked signs is a great start. But people are moved and inspired by people, not signs. So, consider having a designated "First-Time Guest Parking" volunteer role. Actually, two people working together is best and, of course, way more fun. These volunteers might even radio to your greeters or guides or ushers inside to "get ready for a family of seven." What a surprise it will be to these guests when an usher greets them and says, "We've found a place where all seven of you can sit together."

· *How can we best serve families with small children or infants?*

Some churches have created a Wagon Brigade to meet families at their vehicles with a wagon and walk with the parents and children in the wagon to the entry doors. This is a great place to recruit younger volunteers (10 years old or older, based on each child's ability to follow safety rules). This is one more way to say, "We are so on fire that you are here. We planned for you and your family."

· *What does our Handicap Parking area look like?*

How many spots would be best for your church based on your demographics? And even if you have a younger crowd attending, many of them have parents or grandparents, so where would they park? And when that extra person arrives and needs a handicap accessible parking spot, what is the next best option?

· *What if we have a community with large trucks?*

Those vehicles present space and safety issues.

Have you ever considered creating a Truckers Row? Many large trucks are best if they are parked by backing into the space. But doing this maneuver can create a logjam, and safety becomes an issue. How intentional (and fun) to have a place for them! And it helps others when they don't have to struggle with not with seeing around these large trucks when parking.

· *What happens if you run out of parking spots?*

YES! That happens. Do you have an "overflow" plan?

As your church grows, consider nearby retail spaces empty on Sunday mornings. This is an opportunity to connect on another level with your surrounding community. People parking in an otherwise unused restaurant parking lot could lead to customers at the restaurants, especially with intentional encouragement from your church, as a way to say "Thank you!"

· *Other best practices*
- All volunteers must wear safety vests and carry a radio (flashlights when appropriate).
- Fun hats in the children's parking area are highly encouraged.
- Sunscreen and hats are not just for the beach. Let's be safe.
- Assist with setting out traffic cones and signage before services and removing after services.

(This means these volunteers are the typically among the first to arrive and the last to leave. So, consider rotating teams and rotating team members for this duty.)

- Smile, wave, make eye contact, and be deliberate in directing or slowing down the drivers.
- Train together on what hand signals and language everyone will use.
- Train across teams so the traffic flow direction is consistent from Sunday to Sunday.
- Call out regularly (you can smile and talk on the radio) to one another: "Fast car with phone in ear approaching;" "Send the gray Toyota to the visitors row;" "Direct the white van to a handicap spot."

Finally, parking team members are the ones that help prepare for and assist during bad weather. Whether it be spreading salt during snow and ice, shoveling snow, carrying umbrellas in the rain, or escorting people to and from their vehicles, the parking team makes sure that everyone enters and exits safely.

See the Parking Team Member job description in Chapter 13.

CHAPTER 8

GREETERS AND GUIDES

A CASE STUDY

THE FRIENDLY PARKING lot attendants helped **Rachel** feel like she'd made the right decision to turn in to the church. As she approached the front door, a volunteer smiled, looked into her eyes, and said, "Welcome!"

No one has ever opened a door for me, Rachel thought later. *I felt so special. Like I belonged here. I definitely made the right decision to give this a try.*

Hospitality volunteer: Discuss or brainstorm with the team the best way for greeters to welcome a guest.

Greeters

We can never forget we are human beings—we need a personal touch or greeting. Someone to look us in the eye and really see us. Greeters are more than someone to say "Hi" or "Welcome." Their role is to guarantee that every person entering the church is seen and that the church is ready to help in any way.

Greeters can accomplish this in several ways and in several places.

· *Outside doors and worship center doors*

There's something special about seeing a person standing outside waiting for you. And then, as you approach, they swing the door wide open—just for you! Yes, it might be cold or hot outside, but remember, being uncomfortable for Christ is often a part of serving him. If the weather is especially harsh, consider rotating team members in 15-minute increments. Provide fans when it's hot and extra hats, gloves, scarves, and hand warmers when it's cold.

Greeters should always be facing in the direction of the people. Before services, this is facing the parking lot. But after services, as people are leaving, greeters face toward the inside.

Limit conversations with other team members. We should not be so engrossed with each other that we miss our chance to truly see and connect with the person walking in the doors. Stand shoulder-to-shoulder with other team members, not nose-to-nose. When we face one another, we can get lost in the conversation. Guests may get ignored or feel like they're interrupting. You always have the opportunity to connect with your fellow teammate outside of serving, but we get only once chance with that first-time visitor.

Hand out bulletins and greet with a "Hi" or "Hello" "Welcome to ___!" And *smile*.

Shaking hands is not required. Take your cue from the guest's body language.

Eye contact is critical. Let people know they are seen.

Remain at your doorpost at least 15 minutes after service begins. No one is ever late to church when we are kingdom minded. They could have turned around and gone home. They could have decided, it's too late, forget it. But instead, they are welcomed with "So glad you are here!" and are met with the gospel as you live out the love of God. God waits for us. God is patient with us. God is ready to meet this visitor, and he's not bound by our schedules or timetables. Our job is simply to help clear the path.

· *Sidewalks*

Having greeters to bridge the connection between the parking lot and inside the building is a game changer. They may help in any one of several ways.

- They are ready to assist those parked in handicap spaces.
- They can lend a hand to a car full of small children.
- They can hand out stickers to small children.
- They can be extra eyes and ears for any unexpected issues.
- They create energy and intentional welcoming.

• *Umbrella brigade*

When it rains, let's pour out the hospitality! Get ready to escort your guests to and from church. Having large umbrellas to cover two people allows for another connection conversation. And if there's an unexpected rainstorm, consider this plan:

Volunteers hand out umbrellas to people to use as they leave.

Parking lot volunteers collect umbrellas as people get in their cars.

Another possibility is an Umbrella Drop-Off Station for people to use as they drive out. Volunteers here retrieve and recycle umbrellas for more guests to use.

CASE STUDIES

ONCE MONIQUE STEPS into the main foyer, she's overwhelmed with not knowing what to do next or where to take her kids.

A volunteer approaches her. "Good morning!" she says with a smile. "I'm Alice, welcome! Can I help in any way?"

"Hi, I'm Monique and well, this is my first time here, and I don't know the rules or where to go."

"Nice to meet you Monique! How old are your children? I would love to show you what we have that is designed just for them."

"Nick is 7 and Sara is 9. But I'm not sure they would be up for going somewhere else."

"Sure, I understand. Hi Nick and Sara. How about if I gave you a quick tour so you can see and decide then?"

Alice walks them to the children's area. One look at the Ping-Pong table and kids their ages, and Nick and Sara want to play. After helping Monique with getting her kids checked in, Alice walks Monique toward the worship center. They stop to get Monique coffee and chat about where Monique is from.

Alice sees Sam, head usher. "Hey Sam! This is Monique and she is here with her two children for the first time!"

"Hi Monique! Looks like you get the best seat in the house! Do you have preference?"

Monique replies, "Not really."

"How about you follow me then." Sam takes her to a group of people he knows love to meet people and introduces them to Monique. She offers a smile and a thank-you and takes a seat with others. She is not alone.

———

LUIS HAS PARKED in the back. He prefers to lay low, but already two people have greeted him with warm "Good morning!" As he approaches the front door, two others are standing there, as if they are waiting just for him. Then they open the door and greet him. "Good morning!"

"What is happening here?" Luis says to himself. "These people are way too friendly. Is somebody paying them?"

Once inside, he feels a little confused. He's not sure where to go or how to find the men's room. A volunteer walks up and says, "Hey! I'm Brian, I don't think we've met."

"Um, I'm sure we haven't, this is my first time here."

"Great! I'm glad you're here! Is there anything I can help you find or answer any questions?"

"Actually, I need to find the men's room."

"Sure, follow me. And hey, if you'd like some coffee, please help yourself right here." As they get near the men's room, Brian adds, "I'd love to meet you after the service to answer any questions you may have. You'll find me right by the Guest Services desk."

Luis thinks, *OK, this is just too good to be true. Let's see how the rest of this day goes.*

> **Hospitality volunteer:** How would you behave or react in situations like these? Discuss this question with others on the Hospitality Ministry Team.

Guides

These volunteers love to meet people and enjoy guiding first-time guests to the children's area, coffee station, restrooms, or the worship center. They stay with the guest, create conversation, connect, and introduce them to others. This team must grow as your church grows. Guides build relationships and trust with guests, as they stay with each family until they are completely settled in the worship center.

Guides remember this motto: "We don't point people to places. We take them there, personally."

Checking in first-time children can be time consuming and sometimes a little intimidating. Guides offer a simple overview of the children's area so the parent and child can actually see how the ministry works. They may even be able to show them where the rooms are and how they're staffed. Parents need to know their children will be in a safe and fun environment. The guide's help can make parents willing to leave their children in the children's area instead of bringing them along to adult worship, where their wiggling and squirming will distract the parents and those around them.

Best practices for Guides

- Escort families to appropriate children's areas, student ministries, adult classes, or restrooms.
- Regularly take tours of the facility, especially as changes happen.
- Intentionally follow-up with guests after the service with a specific meeting area such as the Guest Services counter.
- Know the basics: Where's the coffee, and is it free, and can it be taken into the worship center? Is anything special happening in the service that day? Baptisms? Classes after services? Celebrations? Sermon topic?
- Assist at doors as needed.

See the Greeter and Guide job description in Chapter 13.

CHAPTER 9

USHERS

CASE STUDIES

AFTER LEAVING THE men's room, **Luis** stands at the back of the Worship Center for most of the first song. It doesn't look like he is waiting for anyone.

The head usher, Sam, approaches Luis. "Hey, good morning!" he says. "I'm Sam. Can I help you find a seat?"

"Ummmm...I'm not sure I'm staying."

"Oh man, I hope so! How can I serve you?"

"What? Oh. Ummm...I've never been here before, but a friend said I should come."

"That's fantastic! I'm so glad you're here! Let's get you the best seat in the house!"

———

JIM AND NANCY WALK in, hand in hand, looking like they belong here. Some people are intimidated by their confidence and good looks, so they don't often have people approach them.

But Sam is on it. He doesn't recognize them, so he introduces himself to them.

They welcome Sam's generous smile and warm greeting. They tell him this is their first time. Sam introduces them to another usher, Charlotte. "Hey Charlotte, this is

Jim and Nancy, and they are looking for two seats on left side."

Charlotte smiles. "So glad you are here!" she says. "Please follow me." As they're seated, she says, "If I can serve you in any way, please don't hesitate to ask. "My name is Charlotte. Thank you for coming today."

A staff person walks in the auditorium, and Sam motions them over. "Hey, a first-time couple was just seated by Charlotte on the left," he says. "I'd love it if you would say hi."

The staff member is able to find Jim and Nancy, shake their hands, and greet them. "Hi, I'm Mary, and I wanted to thank you for visiting us today! I'd love for you stop by the VIP Tent after services to see how we can best serve you!"

Hospitality volunteer: How would you behave or react in situations like these? Discuss this question with others on the Hospitality Ministry Team.

Ushers

*U*shers create a welcoming, distraction-free environment so that people can hear a life-changing message. This role is for those who love to intentionally engage those entering the auditorium.

Best practices for Ushers

- Ushers serve also as greeters and are intentional about welcoming attendees.
- Have small flashlights to assist when lights are low or too dark. Make sure that the flashlights are always pointing straight down.

- Walk to the top of the aisle to greet the guests and escort them to available seating, or provide a "warm handoff" to another usher.
- Pass/serve Communion and offering trays, if applicable. Many churches have a separate team that takes care of this.
- Take attendance.
- Make sure you know where medical teams or those in the congregation who are medically trained are seated and introduce yourself to them.
- Get to know your church's security team and make them aware of any situation that sets off a red flag. If there is no security team presence, be ready to act should the need arise.
- Get to know the worship production team members (sound board operator, etc.). Break down silos and become one team inside the worship center. Serving them first is a great first step. Offer to bring them coffee.
- The doors are to be opened only by the direction of the head usher.
- Know the location of emergency exit doors and have ushers stationed near them.
- Be mindful of handicap seating areas and allow for extra seats reserved for those attending with them.
- As the auditorium begins to fill up, move to assist people with seating. Be mindful of where available seating remains.
- Encourage people to sit toward the front, even though there may be adequate seating elsewhere, but never force them.
- Encourage people to move toward the middle of

each row.

- Find those already sitting in the middle of a row and thank them.
- Remain at your aisle position through the beginning of service; people will come late.
- Close the doors just as the service begins.
- Guard the doors and do not allow people to enter or leave during special times (i.e. prayer times, dramas, transitions, solo performances, videos, etc.). Seat guests as soon as the special feature is finished.
- Silently discourage attendees from walking, exiting, or talking during prayer times.

End of service

- Thank people for coming as they leave their seats, and be ready to help guests in any way.
- Clean up assigned areas by walking down each row and collecting trash or items left behind.
- Take lost items to Guest Services.
- Provide a head count to the person who records attendance.
- Between services, attend a brief usher meeting before the doors are opened for the next service, creating a culture of healthy feedback and "Let's make it better together!"

See the Usher job description in Chapter 13.

CHAPTER 10

SECTION HOSTS

A CASE STUDY

JIM AND NANCY have settled in and are waiting for the service to start. They wanted to get in early to make sure they didn't miss anything.

Ray walks to his seat in the row in front of Jim and Nancy. As he settles in, he looks around and notices they are a couple he doesn't know.

"Hey, I'm Ray. I don't think we've met!"

"Hi, I'm Jim and this is my wife, Nancy. We are actually visiting for the first time."

"Wonderful! It's a pleasure to meet you both, and I get to welcome you to our church! If you don't mind sharing, what brought you here today?"

"Sure. We just thought we would check out this church today. Some co-workers mentioned this church, so here we are. Do you happen to know Steve Jones or Sally Smith?"

"I don't think so. But I can say we are truly glad you decided to join us. The sermon series we are in is all about prayer, and I know this is something I can always get better at. If I can serve you both in any way or if you have any questions after the service, please don't hesitate to let me know."

"Thanks Ray!"

They shake hands and sit down. Jim and Nancy turn to one another and smile. They're grateful they didn't have to sit with that awkward feeling of being outsiders at church.

Hospitality volunteer: How would you behave or react in a situation like this? Discuss this question with others on the Hospitality Ministry Team.

Section Hosts

*T*his may be a relatively new role for most churches. But it's a really simple, and perhaps one of the most impactful and personal ways we can connect with those attending church with us.

One of the top reasons people say they would not return to a church is, "No one welcomed me." "No one even spoke to me while I was sitting for more than five minutes waiting for the service to start."

Being greeted in the parking lot or at the door isn't enough. Imagine sitting in a new space, and everyone else seems to know one another while you're ignored. It takes you back to your middle school lunchroom—where you sat alone, feeling awkward amid a sea of people laughing and talking with each other but not with you.

This role is for your friendliest people. The section host enjoys meeting people to make them feel genuinely welcomed. He or she is at ease with asking noninvasive questions and sharing a little about the church.

The section host makes sure anyone he doesn't know or hasn't met is greeted and engaged. Those serving in other roles can be a section host when they are simply attending a church service.

And there's a wonderful side benefit when church members see the section host regularly greeting newcomers or strangers. The welcoming spirit becomes contagious. The ministry of the section host can create a radical hospitality culture in the entire church.

Best practices for Section Hosts

- Sit in a different place every Sunday. This ensures you get to meet new people.
- Be open to talking to people who are not like you.
- Don't assume anyone is single. Sometimes just a wife or a husband will attend a new church before the other spouse attends.
- Be ready with easy ways to start conversations. Learn how to overcome your fear that someone is a regular attendee, but you think they're a visitor.

Here are sample Section Hosts conversation starters:

"Good morning! I'm Evan, I don't think we've met." (This works even if you're meeting a longtime member for the first time.)

After that, the conversation could go a couple of different ways, for example:

GUEST: Good morning, I'm Sally. It's nice to meet you too.

SH: I can't believe it's so cold/hot today! I'm from the south/north and this is way too cold for me!

Other possibilities for easy conversation include the calendar ("Can you believe it's already Christmas? Or Thanksgiving? Or summer?") or sports ("Are you a baseball fan? Did you see the game last night?").

Do NOT *ever* ask, "Is this your first time here?" Instead, the conversation could go something like this:

SH: So how long have you been attending our church?

GUEST: We've been coming here for about three years.

SH: Great! I'm so glad we got to meet. We've/I've been attending for about two years.

GUEST: Well, actually, not three years consistently. We travel a lot.

SH: Oh traveling. I'd love to hear about that.

If the guest is a first-timer, the conversation might go something like this:

SH: So how long have you been attending our church?

GUEST: It's our first time. We just moved here from Buffalo. (Guests will often explain why they're newcomers.)

SH: Welcome! How did you find out about us? (Or) What brought you here from Buffalo? (Or) What brought you to our church today?

This is the critical time to simply LISTEN! People will tell you their why or what they are looking for if you lean in and listen, rather than trying to tell them about the latest group or event at your church.

See the Section Host job description in Chapter 13.

CHAPTER 11

AFTER THE SERVICE AND WELCOME DESK HOSTS

CASE STUDIES

As **Luis** walks out of the service, he remembers that guy he met who said he'd meet him afterwards. "He seemed like a friendly guy, and I am here to figure out if I can find friends here. But I don't remember his name. Oh yeah, he said to meet him somewhere...ah, there it is, Guest Services."

Brian spots Luis walking toward him and moves to meet him. "Hey Luis, great to see you again!

Luis notices Bryan's name badge (whew!) "This guy remembered my name, at least I get some help with his name badge. Oh, hey, Brian."

"So how was the service? You can be honest with me. We always want to get better, and we know every church isn't for everyone. We're just glad you came today."

"Well, the service was fine. I really resonated with the message."

"That's good to hear! I would love to hear more of your thoughts on that. We actually have a men's group that discusses each message at their meeting the following week. If you're interested, I can help you find it. Or I'm happy to give you my contact information if you have any questions."

"Sure, I'd like a little more information on the men's group."

Brian invites Luis to a laptop and pulls up the church's GROUP webpage. He explains more about their groups and asks Luis a few simple questions.

"We know that simply joining a new group, without knowing anyone, can be intimidating. So here are a few options for you to check out. Are there particular days of the week that are best for you?"

Luis leaves the church building with a sense of being seen and valued. He has connected with another person close to his age and learned about options for taking some next steps. To him, it looks like it was worth going today and maybe even returning next week.

MONIQUE WAS PLEASANTLY surprised that meeting people for the first time was easier than she imagined.

But as she walks out of the service, she realizes she's a little confused about where to go to pick up her kids. She notices the Guest Services area and thinks surely someone there could help her, even if it feels a little awkward to ask.

As she heads toward the Guest Services area, Alice walks up (because Alice was actually looking for Monique). "Hey Monique! How are you doing?"

"Well, this is embarrassing, but I forget which direction to go get my kids."

"That's totally normal. It can be disorienting when visiting a new place. I can take you there."

Monique leaves not feeling judged, and even more, a sense that there are other people out there who really want to help her. This was easier than she thought.

Hospitality volunteer: How would you behave or react in situations like these? Discuss this question with others on the Hospitality Ministry Team.

Welcome Desk Host

Think of this area as a "Grand Central Station," where volunteers can tell guests they'll meet them after each service. The most important, nonnegotiable part is having the right people serving here. Volunteers should be able to answer questions and provide basic information about the church. You don't have to know all the answers, but this role is for someone who can easily talk to new people, provide suggestions, ask questions, and be okay with saying, "I don't know that answer, but I can find out!"

Also, most churches are providing access to the church's website with information about current events and sign-ups for small groups or classes. So volunteers serving here need to be comfortable with using a computer, laptop, or iPad.

Since many guests will be pointed to this space, the area should be clean, inviting, clutter-free, bright, and obvious. Make sure it is maintained with only current information. We may have only a minute to make a connection with someone, so this area should be the easiest and most comfortable place to meet people.

It can be intimidating to walk up to a group of people, especially if they are behind a large counter. We've seen this done many creative ways, such as low counters that wrap around in an oval to kiosks or simply tall cafe tables that hold a laptop and pens.

Best practices for Welcome Desk Hosts

- Ideally, though this may vary due to church size, this post requires at least two people to remain at the Welcome Desk throughout the services, in addition to between services.

- Supplies should be stored and available here (such as earplugs, offering envelopes, connect cards, pens, mints, etc.).
- Area should be clutter free. No outside flyers.
- Consider keeping a FUN BOX labeled "For Children" here. It might contain stickers, a coloring page, or snacks (given only with the permission of the parent, of course).
- Medical teams check in here and get lanyards and/ or radios.
- Be mindful and intentional that this area is not a hangout for volunteers and friends.

See the Welcome Desk Host job description in Chapter 13.

On the Way to the Car

A FINAL CASE STUDY

As **Luis, Monique**, **Rachel**, and **Jim and Nancy** start out of the building, they notice it's raining. It seems the weatherman got it wrong when he predicted only a slight chance of rain today.

A volunteer walks up to each of them and offers an umbrella.

"Hi, please feel free to use this umbrella, and a volunteer will meet you at your vehicle to retrieve it. Or you can simply drop it off at the Umbrella Station as you drive out."

As they leave, each of them thinks something similar:

"Who are these people? This is as good, if not better, than any treatment at a fancy hotel or restaurant! It was a good idea to come to this church today. I look forward to coming back next week!"

Hospitality volunteer: how would you behave or react in a situation like this? Discuss this question with others on the Hospitality Ministry Team.

SECTION 3

HOSPITALITY MINISTRY TOOLS

*T*his section is a toolbox of practical helps and ideas. Utilize the following tips and information to be encouraged and equipped, as you demonstrate and share the love of Christ to the guests you welcome to you church.

CHAPTER 12

THE PRESERVICE HUDDLE

*G*ather your team together before they serve. Look them in the eye, encourage them, pray with them, and remind them that today could be someone's first Sunday.

WHY We Huddle

Before every football game, the coach draws the team together to focus on the task at hand and pump them up.

Jesus was constantly huddling his disciples. He listened to them, taught them, encouraged them, and redirected them. He didn't expect them to serve well just because he had explained how several months earlier.

Our task is just as challenging as a football game. Our ministry is crucial to the kingdom. Our service is an extension of the mission Jesus created with his disciples when he was on earth. If they needed gatherings to focus their hearts and grow their minds in his ways, so do we.

Huddling is a form of training, not the type of training that gives the dos and don'ts, but the kind that equips and empowers volunteers to accomplish God's work and will.

In the huddle, we challenge each other to rely on God for that day's service. We remember the wisdom of Proverbs 3:9-10 (MSG):

"Trust God from the bottom of your heart; don't try to figure out everything on your own. Listen for God's voice in everything you do, everywhere you go; he's the one who will keep you on track. Don't assume that you know it all. Run to God! Run from evil! Your body will glow with health, your very bones will vibrate with life! Honor God with everything you own; give him the first and the best. Your barns will burst, your wine vats will brim over."

We huddle because we can't figure out everything on our own! All kinds of unexpected situations can happen on a Sunday. We need the grace of Jesus and clarity from our ministry leader—as much of both as possible!

In the midst of our Sunday morning service, it'll be harder to hear the voice of God if we aren't intentional about first tuning into the voice of God before we get started. When we tune in, we receive grace so we can extend grace, with a supernatural awareness of when it's needed.

As the *First* Impressions ministry, we must give him our *firsts* so we'll be ready for all the "brimming over" of blessing God has in store for us to experience. We all want our church "barns" bursting. We want to make disciples and disciple-makers. But we must *first* be discipled.

Here's what happens if we rush through the morning and slack on communing with God, carrying each other's burdens to the foot of the cross, or equipping our people with the tools they need to be confident and successful in the work at hand: we quickly, deliberately, and unfortunately take ministry out of our service and turn it to duty. We quickly go from being Mary's *abiding* with Jesus to Martha's *doing* for Jesus (see Luke 10:38-42).

We must *abide* before we *do*.

We must *abide* to sanctify what we *do*.

This is why we huddle.

The WHAT of a Huddle

Volunteers best serve potential guests by being at their posts 30 minutes before service; therefore, Huddles take place 10-15 minutes before your volunteers go to their service posts. Although Huddles do not take long, they are key to setting the tone for the day.

Components of a Huddle include:
- Opening prayer
- Acknowledgements/praises/celebrations of volunteers
- Information about the day/service(s)
- Devotional time/worship
- Closing prayer and send off

CHAPTER 13

HOSPITALITY MINISTRY
JOB DESCRIPTIONS

$\mathcal{T}$he following pages include job descriptions for several positions that you may have as part of a Hospitality Ministry Team. Depending on the size of your church, you may or may not have all of the below roles, and the number of people in each role may also vary.

Having a job description on hand for your role can be a handy point of reference.

Here is a list of the job descriptions included in this chapter:
- Hospitality Ministry/First Impressions Coordinator
- Team Leader
- Parking Team Member
- Welcome Desk Host
- Greeter and Guide
- Usher
- Section Host

Hospitality Ministry/First Impressions Coordinator Job Description

DEFINITION

The First Impressions Coordinator is responsible for the attendee experience—from the parking lot to the seat in the auditorium and all points between. The FI Coordinator is also responsible for creating and promoting a culture of discipleship, biblical hospitality, and volunteers that "wow" guests with their service by providing vision and direction to the Parking, Greeter, Coffee, Usher, and Follow-Up teams for main Sunday gatherings.

PURPOSE

The First Impressions Coordinator exists to lead the First Impressions team by modeling best practices, investing in their team, and training up leaders and volunteers who serve from a heart of grace and empowerment to show attendees Jesus through their service.

STRATEGY

Organize volunteer teams and leaders and provide ongoing trainings and vision casting.

GOAL

The goal is for people to leave after their encounter with us saying, "It's as if they knew I was coming." You want to leave them thinking, "Wow! What just happened?" When you think of your smile and handshake as a difference maker in someone's day, you suddenly realize that tending even to small details can make a big difference.

The goal of the First Impressions Coordinator is to develop leaders and a culture of exceptional biblical hospitality. Develop your team so that members grow into a missional community.

TEAM RESPONSIBILITIES

To eliminate any barrier that might keep people from hearing the message and receiving Jesus as their Lord and Savior so that they can move life forward toward God's best. With that goal in mind, the First Impressions Coordinator will:

- Cast vision for the purpose of this ministry.
- Develop and manage a process to recruit, train, and multiply volunteers.
- Train up team leaders for each area of this ministry.
- Schedule volunteers each week and, ultimately, share that responsibility with the team leaders.
- Ensure each volunteer has a cleared background check.
- Ensure there are safety protocols in place that the team knows how to execute in case of an emergency.
- Encourage team leaders and volunteers and develop community within the team.
- Manage and organize the inventory and storage of all coffee supplies on a weekly basis.
- Manage and organize all inventory pertaining to the needs of the hospitality team.
- Update all scheduled host team volunteers each week with key information pertaining to the church.
- Manage the process for first-time and second-time visitor follow-up with clear next steps for them to take.

Team Leader Job Description

DEFINITION

The Team Leader is the lead of a specific area of the First Impressions Ministry; they help with organization and cultivation of a culture of biblical hospitality as a whole. There is a Parking Lot Team Leader, a Greeter Team Leader, a Section Host Team Leader, an Usher Team Leader, and a Welcome Desk Team Leader. As other teams are created to facilitate First Impressions, each team will have its own Team Leader.

PURPOSE

The Team Leader exists to allow for organization and community building within in the First Impressions Ministry.

STRATEGY

The Team Leader will report to the First Impressions Coordinator, meeting with them monthly, and then meeting with their own team when necessary. The Team Leader is the point person for the volunteers on their team to provide logistics and also spiritual depth to the volunteers' service.

GOAL

We want to be the most hospitable place on earth! As a service leader, you play a big part in this by organizing and equipping your volunteers.

TEAM RESPONSIBILITIES

To eliminate any barrier that might keep people from hearing the message and receiving Jesus as their Lord and Savior so that they can move life forward toward God's best. With that goal in mind, the First Impressions Team Leader will:

- Encourage team members in conversation and with thank-you notes.
- Model best practices.
- Treat your volunteer team as a small group.
- Celebrate the wins with your team along the way (especially when a team member goes above and beyond).
- Continually build up and train one or two of your team members to be the next Team Leader.
- Lead the logistics (scheduling, materials needed, information needed, etc.) of your team for Sundays.
- Appropriately place the team members of your team for Sundays.
- Recruit and train new volunteers for your service.
- Communicate with the Hospitality Ministry/First Impressions Coordinator.
- Attend all meetings and trainings.

Parking Team Member Job Description

DEFINITION

The Parking Team is more than just directing and parking cars. The team is an integral part of helping guests feel welcome the minute they pull into the parking lot.

PURPOSE

The Parking Team exists to create a warm atmosphere in the parking lot. They want to make people feel comfortable enough to get out of their cars and attend service, in order for them to experience their encounter with Jesus.

STRATEGY

Be genuine in your connection. Smile, wave, give high-fives, and walk first-time guests to the greeters at the door. This helps every team to be able to recognize who our first-time guests are.

GOAL

One of the biggest barriers someone can have is feeling too afraid to walk through the doors. This is why the Parking Team is so important. We are our church's first impression our guests experience. Remember, your smile and friendly greeting can make a big difference in someone's day.

TEAM RESPONSIBILITIES

To eliminate any barrier that would keep people from getting out of their cars and coming to service, hearing the message, and receiving Jesus as their Lord and Savior so that they can move life forward toward God's best. With that goal in mind, Parking Lot Team Members will:

BEFORE THE SERVICE

- Set up parking lot cones, blocking, and directional signs *before* the Preservice Huddle.
- If your parking lot is especially large, you may use golf carts to transport guests from the farthest spots to the church building's front doors. If so, make sure your golf carts are at the front of the building ready to roll, and be sure to verify that they are fully charged.
- Set up cones.
- Grab vests, signal wands, rain coats, etc.
- Place VIP (First-Time Guest) Parking signs at the entrance directing our first-time guests to the parking spots.

AS YOU SERVE

- Maintain a smile at all times.
- Make guests feel welcomed and honored.
- Keep them dry. (Have umbrellas ready for guests as well as a towel to dry the golf cart seats.)
- Clearly direct people to the next available spot.
- Keep golf carts free of trash.
- Welcome first-time guests.
- Let parents know that we have incredible children's and student ministries, with a team of people who prepared all week to create age-appropriate services just for them.

Welcome Desk Host Job Description

DEFINITION

The Welcome Desk Team is an integral part of answering guests' questions and connecting guests to the life of the church, in order for them to move their lives forward toward God's best.

PURPOSE

These interactions are vital for people to gain a clearer understanding of who we are as a church, what opportunities we have for them, and how to enjoy their visit. The Welcome Desk also serves as the "lost and found," part of security, and as a central place for guests to connect and get an idea of next steps.

STRATEGY

To create a comfortable space with familiar faces that can meet as many needs of the guest as possible so that guests can easily connect with the church and find their next steps into our church community.

GOAL

Discover and eliminate the barriers preventing guests from having a positive experience at our church. These include the physical ("Where is the auditorium? Where are the restrooms? Where should my children go?) and the spiritual (I want to know how to become a Christian. I'm interested in joining a small group.). Remember, your smile and friendly greeting can make a big difference in someone's day.

TEAM RESPONSIBILITIES

To eliminate any barrier that might keep people from connecting with our church before or after hearing the message, especially if they've received Jesus as their Lord and Savior so that they can move life forward toward God's best. With that goal in mind:

- Attend the Preservice Huddle.
- Maintain a smile at all times.
- Keep the Welcome Desk neat and orderly so guests can clearly see the information available.
- Have the first-time guest gifts ready.
- Refrain from texting, eating, chewing gum, etc. while at your post.
- Stay at your post the entire service to answer any guest questions throughout the morning.
- Stay informed about what is going on at church and where main rooms are (i.e. the restrooms, coffee, kids and student rooms, etc.).
- Make guests feel welcomed and honored.
- Walk guests to where they need to go.
- Clearly direct people to their next step in your church's assimilation process.
- Let parents know that we have incredible children's and student ministries, led by teams who prepared all week to create age-appropriate services just for them.
- Make sure guests fill out a Connection Card.

HANDLING DIFFICULT SITUATIONS

Remember, safety is a priority, for both the guest and the team member. Here are some guidelines to follow.

• *Pay close attention to body language.* If you are feeling uneasy, there is probably a reason. Bring others into the conversation.

· *Connect with those of your own gender.* Men connect with other men, and women connect with other women. If you find yourself in a situation where you are the only open person and someone of the opposite gender approaches you, help them but try to bring another person into the conversation as well.

• *Be very careful about giving your contact information.* Do not feel pressured to give more information than you would like.

· *Work together.* Be ready to contact your Team Lead, who will connect with your church's security team (should you have one), or your head usher and/or your executive pastor.

· *If anyone looks suspicious* (For example: wandering around the parking lot, looking in cars, loitering in the hallways, appears to have a weapon, carrying a suitcase or backpack, etc.), connect with your Team Lead and the security team (if you have one) first, in order to evaluate the situation as a team.

· *Know how to respond to benevolence requests.* If anyone is seeking financial help of any kind, contact your Team Lead. They will know the person to contact to find resources in the community. Contact your Head Usher and/or security team if the person becomes argumentative or displays suspicious behavior.

Greeter and Guide Job Description

DEFINITION

Our Greeting Team creates a welcoming atmosphere that engages guests in a way that honors them, sets them at ease, and demonstrates the love of Christ.

PURPOSE

The Greeting Team exists to guide and direct people as they begin their experience here every weekend.

STRATEGY

The Greeting Team members offer the smile and warm handshake that puts our guests at ease as they arrive at our walkway and front doors.

GOAL

The goal is for people to leave after their encounter with us saying, "Wow! It's as if they knew I was coming." Remember, your smile and friendly greeting can make a big difference in someone's day.

TEAM RESPONSIBILITIES

- Welcome and engage guests in the front of the campus, changing your position based on the number of guests arriving at different areas.
- Make a fantastic first impression.
- Make opportunities to honor guests by opening car doors, carrying baby carriers, holding an umbrella over a guest when it is raining, etc.

- While you are positioned at the doors, engage and greet every guest as they enter while also watching for first-time guests. If you see a first-time guest, let your Team Leader know so they can help show them around before service starts. Prop open and close doors as prompted by the Team Leader.
- Escort guests with kids to the children's check-in area, making sure they are being greeted and directed by the Children's Team. Let them know that we have incredible children's and student teams who have been working all week to prepare age-relevant services.
- Be ready to lead guests to areas they may be seeking: restrooms, children's area, auditorium, etc.
- Be sure to stay in position until released, which is about 15 minutes after the service begins.
- Attend the Preservice Huddle.

Usher Job Description

DEFINITION

An usher is more than someone who shows a guest to their seat. The Usher Team is an integral part of providing an exciting, inviting, and spiritually uplifting service.

PURPOSE

The Usher Team exists to create the atmosphere and eliminate any barrier so that people can connect and receive all that God has in store for them.

STRATEGY

Create and ensure a distraction-free worship experience for everyone.

GOAL

The goal is for people to leave after their encounter with us saying, "Wow! It's as if they knew I was coming." Remember, your smile and friendly greeting can make a big difference in someone's day.

TEAM RESPONSIBILITIES

To eliminate any barrier that might keep people from hearing the message and receiving Jesus as their Lord and Savior so that they can move life forward toward God's best. With that goal in mind:

- All ushers remain on duty until all guests are seated.
- Assist all guests to fill all seats from the center first, then to the outside of each row.

- Greet families with small children and recommend the appropriate children's ministry.
- During the service, two ushers should remain at the main doors and two ushers at the side aisles to aid in minimizing distractions.
- At the end of each service, prepare the auditorium for the next service by picking up trash and replacing chairs as needed.
- Remove anyone causing a loud disturbance. If they refuse, contact your Team Leader and the Security Team, if you have one.
- Please connect with your Team Leader and the Security Team first, in order to evaluate the situation as a team. (Ex: walking toward the stage, appears to have a weapon, standing during service, carrying in a suitcase or backpack)
- Attend the Preservice Huddle.

POSITION ROLES

DOOR USHERS

- Open all doors at the same time (15 minutes prior to start of service).
- Seat potential distractions near the exits.
- Greet guests with energy and enthusiasm as they enter.
- Smile and make eye contact.
- Hold guests in the lobby during prayer.
- Stay aware of available seats and escort guests to them.
- Provide escort for distractions and people leaving the auditorium to the lobby.

- Remain at the door to prevent it from closing loudly during service.

MIDDLE USHERS

- Greet guests with energy and enthusiasm as they come in the auditorium.
- Smile and make eye contact.
- *Always* face incoming guests as rows fill.
- Get party count from guests as rows fill.
- Fill every seat in a row, trying to leave none empty. Fill in center first then move to sides.
- Ask people to move in to fill gaps. Go back to fill in ones and twos whenever possible.
- While the last row is filling, communicate the number of open seats to the door usher.
- Place and remove the podium during the transitions for Pastor/Communicators, if you don't have stage managers who do this.

ATTENDANCE COUNT

Attendance must be counted the following areas:
- Auditorium Seats (Left, Center, and Right sections)
- Pastor/Communicators
- Production Booth
- Ushers
- Lobby/Foyer
- All main rooms other than the auditorium (such as a coffee shop or café)
- Children's ministry
- Student ministry
- Any adult ministry classes taking place
- Parking lot

OFFERING AND CLOSING

- Please pay attention to the cues for being in place. Proceed as directed by your Team Lead/service plan.
- Hand offering bucket to the first person in the row beginning in the front. Then return to retrieve the buckets from the end of the opposite section. Keep an eye on the buckets for any suspicious behavior.
- The Team Lead will place all monies in the safe. Any money collected outside of the offering time should be given to the Team Lead.
- As service ends and guests are dismissed, the ushers will open all doors so that guests may depart the auditorium. Smile and thank guests for coming.

COMMUNION

- Complete any preparation necessary.
- Check to make sure you have enough supplies to complete communion for the congregation.
- Serve with reverence.
- Always serve the bread before the juice.
- Go to your position and serve until all have received the elements.
- Pass the elements down each aisle and collect the trays or cups after the observance is over.
- Clean up any trash or cups left over after the service is over.

SECURITY

- No stage access to anyone outside the worship team, communicators, or stage hands.

- Be friendly yet intimidating. Be able to take action, if necessary, by talking to your Team Lead and a member of the Security Team, if you have one.
- Know where all fire alarms and fire extinguishers are located.
- Note where all emergency exits are. Familiarize yourself with the surrounding area just outside the auditorium so you can help with evacuation of one or hundreds of people.
- Your Team Lead will have direct connection to our Security Team. Let them know if you become aware of any safety or security issues.
- Reserved aisle seats are for members we are familiar with, who will act as a barrier and first line of defense should someone in the aisle want to create a disruption or rush the platform.
- Make note of who your Security Team members are for the weekend so you will know who is available should a medical or security need arise.

Section Host Job Description

DEFINITION

Section Hosts are the greeters of the worship center and work alongside the ushers to create a fun, welcoming, efficient, and worshipful environment for the guest.

PURPOSE

The Section Hosts exist to make sure guests experience connection and care before the worship service begins.

STRATEGY

Genuinely making connections with the people in your section by engaging them in friendly conversation and being attentive to needs (spiritual as well as physical).

GOAL

Section Hosts are key to helping guests feel noticed, valued, and cared for.

TEAM RESPONSIBILITIES

OWN YOUR SECTION

As a Section Host, you are one of the last contacts a person has before the start of our service. Remember to be in your section thirty minutes before the service begins to ensure you can meet as many people as possible. Be ready to be used by God to offer welcome, encouragement, or a word of truth to someone you meet.

- Make sure your section is comfortable and clean.
- Create a warm and welcoming environment.

- Get to know the names of the guests in your section. Be willing to hear prayer requests.
- Attend the Preservice Huddle.

SERVE YOUR SECTION

• *Be aware of needs.* Guests in your section may need:

- Water or a mint
- A Bible
- A pen
- A bulletin or Connection Card
- Information
- Assistance

• *Be sensitive.* There will be times when we need to leave people alone. They may be struggling with sin or sorrow and are not willing to open up to you. If you sense they do not want to engage with you, that's OK. Smile and let them have space.

• *Be prepared.* As a host, you are a good set of eyes on the people entering our sanctuary.

Look for people who need some help. They might need a bulletin, a tissue, or a bottle of water. Serve them by getting them what they need.

Look for people who might need prayer. (Ask if you can pray with and for them. Preferably, guys pray with guys and ladies pray with ladies. If that doesn't work out, grab someone else to pray with you.)

Look for people who appear disgruntled or suspicious. If you do see this, please get someone on the Security Team.

• *Be flexible.* Until we have all our sections full of team members, feel free to roam.

Always be solution minded with a smile on your face, no matter what the situation. The most important thing is the guest and making them feel comfortable.

CHAPTER 14

HOW TO REMEMBER NAMES

*H*ere are some tips to help improve your name recall:

- Listen carefully as they tell you their name. If you don't understand them, ask them to say it again. This communicates interest.
- Pay attention to the name and face. Look the person in the eye and say their name back to them. For example, "It's so nice to meet you, Bob."
- Associate the name with an image.
- Take a mental snapshot of their name and face and say their name again as you say goodbye.
- Meditation improves your working memory.
- Drinking coffee (believe it or not) improves your memory, so have some coffee when you gather before your worship service.
- Eating berries improves your long-term memory.
- Exercising (always a good thing) improves your memory.
- Chewing gum helps to make stronger memories but beware of chewing in an obnoxious and noticeable manner.
- A good night's sleep will not only help improve your memory but will help you be at your best.
- Last but not least, wear and use name badges.

CHAPTER 15

HOSPITALITY SCRIPTURES

*M*ay the following Bible passages be an encouragement to you as you serve others.

So reach out and welcome one another to God's glory. Jesus did it; now you do it! Jesus, staying true to God's purposes, reached out in a special way to the Jewish insiders so that the old ancestral promises would come true for them. As a result, the non-Jewish outsiders have been able to experience mercy and to show appreciation to God. Just think of all the Scriptures that will come true in what we do! For instance:

Then I'll join outsiders in a hymn-sing; I'll sing to your name!

And this one: Outsiders and insiders, rejoice together!

And again: People of all nations, celebrate God!

All colors and races, give hearty praise!

And Isaiah's word: There's the root of our ancestor Jesse, breaking through the earth and growing tree tall, Tall enough for everyone everywhere to see and take hope!

Oh! May the God of green hope fill you up with joy, fill you up with peace, so that your believing lives, filled with the life-giving energy of the Holy Spirit, will brim over with hope! (Romans 15:7-13, MSG).

"A new command I give you: Love one another. As I have loved you, so you must love one another. By this everyone will know that you are my disciples, if you love one another" (John 13:34-35).

When a stranger sojourns with you in your land, you shall not do him wrong. You shall treat the stranger who sojourns with you as the native among you, and you shall love him as yourself, for you were strangers in the land of Egypt: I am the Lord your God (Leviticus 19:33-34, ESV).

All the believers were together and had everything in common. They sold property and possessions to give to anyone who had need (Acts 2:44-45).

There was an estate nearby that belonged to Publius, the chief official of the island. He welcomed us to his home and showed us generous hospitality for three days (Acts 28:7).

Since an overseer manages God's household, he must be blameless—not overbearing, not quick-tempered, not given to drunkenness, not violent, not pursuing dishonest gain. Rather, he must be hospitable, one who loves what is good, who is self-controlled, upright, holy and disciplined (Titus 1:7-8).

Now the overseer is to be above reproach, faithful to his wife, temperate, self-controlled, respectable, hospitable, able to teach (1 Timothy 3:2).

Keep on loving one another as brothers and sisters. Do not forget to show hospitality to strangers, for by so doing some people have shown hospitality to angels without knowing it. ... And do not forget to do good and to share with others, for with such sacrifices God is pleased (Hebrews 13:1-2, 16).

The Lord appeared to Abraham near the great trees of Mamre while he was sitting at the entrance to his tent in the heat of the day. Abraham looked up and saw three men standing nearby. When he saw them, he hurried from the entrance of his tent to meet them and bowed low to the ground.
He said, "If I have found favor in your eyes, my lord, do not pass your servant by. Let a little water be brought, and then you may all wash your feet and rest under this tree. Let me get you something to eat, so you can be refreshed and then go on your way—now that you have come to your servant."

"Very well," they answered, "do as you say."

So Abraham hurried into the tent to Sarah. "Quick," he said, "get three seahs of the finest flour and knead it and bake some bread."

Then he ran to the herd and selected a choice, tender calf and gave it to a servant, who hurried to prepare it. He then brought some curds and milk and the calf that had been prepared, and set these before them. While they ate, he stood near them under a tree (Genesis 18:1-8).

For we are God's handiwork, created in Christ Jesus to do good works, which God prepared in advance for us to do (Ephesians 2:10).

Whoever oppresses the poor shows contempt for their Maker, but whoever is kind to the needy honors God (Proverbs 14:31).

Whoever is kind to the poor lends to the Lord, and he will reward them for what they have done (Proverbs 19:17).

But when you give a banquet, invite the poor, the crippled, the lame, the blind (Luke 14:13).

"Teacher, which is the greatest commandment in the Law?"

Jesus replied: "'Love the Lord your God with all your heart and with all your soul and with all your mind.' This is the first and greatest commandment. And the second is like it: 'Love your neighbor as yourself.' All the Law and the Prophets hang on these two commandments (Matthew 22:36-40).

On one occasion an expert in the law stood up to test Jesus. "Teacher," he asked, "what must I do to inherit eternal life?"

"What is written in the Law?" he replied. "How do you read it?"

He answered, "'Love the Lord your God with all your heart and with all your soul and with all your strength and with all your mind'; and, 'Love your neighbor as yourself.'"

"You have answered correctly," Jesus replied. *"Do this and you will live."*

But he wanted to justify himself, so he asked Jesus, *"And who is my neighbor?"*

In reply Jesus said: *"A man was going down from Jerusalem to Jericho, when he was attacked by robbers. They stripped him of his clothes, beat him and went away, leaving him half dead. A priest happened to be going down the same road, and when he saw the man, he passed by on the other side. So too, a Levite, when he came to the place and saw him, passed by on the other side. But a Samaritan, as he traveled, came where the man was; and when he saw him, he took pity on him. He went to him and bandaged his wounds, pouring on oil and wine. Then he put the man on his own donkey, brought him to an inn and took care of him. The next day he took out two denarii and gave them to the innkeeper. 'Look after him,' he said, 'and when I return, I will reimburse you for any extra expense you may have.'*

"Which of these three do you think was a neighbor to the man who fell into the hands of robbers?"

The expert in the law replied, *"The one who had mercy on him."*

Jesus told him, *"Go and do likewise"* (Matthew 25:34-36).

Share with the Lord's people who are in need. Practice hospitality (Romans 12:13).

Offer hospitality to one another without grumbling (1 Peter 4:9).

The King will reply, 'Truly I tell you, whatever you did for one of the least of these brothers and sisters of mine, you did for me' (Matthew 25:40).

Dear friend, you are faithful in what you are doing for the brothers and sisters, even though they are strangers to you. They have told the church about your love. Please send them on their way in a manner that honors God. It was for the sake of the Name that they went out, receiving no help from the pagans. We ought therefore to show hospitality to such people so that we may work together for the truth (3 John 5-8).

As you read over what I have written to you, you'll be able to see for yourselves into the mystery of Christ. None of our ancestors understood this. Only in our time has it been made clear by God's Spirit through his holy apostles and prophets of this new order. The mystery is that people who have never heard of God and those who have heard of him all their lives (what I've been calling outsiders and insiders) stand on the same ground before God. They get the same offer, same help, same promises in Christ Jesus. The Message is accessible and welcoming to everyone, across the board (Ephesians 3:4-6, MSG).

The end of all things is near. Therefore be alert and of sober mind so that you may pray. Above all, love each other deeply, because love covers over a multitude of sins. Offer hospitality to one another without grumbling. Each of you should use whatever gift you have received to serve others, as faithful stewards of God's grace in its various forms. If anyone speaks, they should do so as one who speaks the very words of God. If anyone serves, they should do so with the strength God provides, so that in all things God may be praised through Jesus Christ. To him be the glory and the power for ever and ever. Amen (1 Peter 4:7-11).

We proclaim to you what we have seen and heard, so that you also may have fellowship with us. And our fellowship is with the Father and with his Son, Jesus Christ (1 John 1:3).

Gaius, whose hospitality I and the whole church here enjoy, sends you his greetings (Romans 16:23).

Whoever serves me must follow me; and where I am, my servant also will be. My Father will honor the one who serves me (John 12:26).

Never be lacking in zeal, but keep your spiritual fervor, serving the Lord. Be joyful in hope, patient in affliction, faithful in prayer. Share with the Lord's people who are in need. Practice hospitality (Romans 12:11-13).

"And whoever wants to be first must be your slave—just as the Son of Man did not come to be served, but to serve, and to give his life as a ransom for many" (Matthew 20:27-28).

Make the most of every opportunity in these evil days (Ephesians 5:16, NLT).

Consequently, faith comes from hearing the message, and the message is heard through the word about Christ (Romans 10:17).

So in everything, do to others what you would have them do to you, for this sums up the Law and the Prophets (Matthew 7:12).

CHAPTER 16

DOS AND DON'TS

Some things you will want to be sure to do:

- Do smile—always!
- Do be at your post thirty minutes before the start of each service time.
- Do look available to help: no drinking or eating while at your post.
- Do be excited to serve God and show it.
- Do make yourself visible and available to welcome guests, answer questions, and maintain the overall friendly environment.
- Do return to your original posts to say good-bye to guests.
- Do help people by opening a door.
- Do go the extra mile.
- Do read body language and be respectful of people's personal space.
- Do be naturally warm.
- Do ask, "How long have you been coming?"

Some things to avoid:

- Don't have anything in your hands when you serve, such as your coffee, phone, coat, or purse.
- Don't lean on furniture or rails.
- Don't frown.

- Don't do the minimum.
- Don't presume a stranger will welcome a hug.
- Don't over-do the greeting.
- Don't say "is this your first time here?"
- Don't just stand there. Remember this short time is not for chatting with friends; stay focused on the opportunity to connect with someone new.
- Don't forget to tidy-up the areas where you serve.

CHAPTER 17

BASIC ETIQUETTE AND APPEARANCE

Etiquette Tips
- When it comes to basic etiquette, remember the Golden Rule:
  "So in everything, do to others what you would have them do to you, for this sums up the Law and the Prophets" (Matthew 7:12).
- Promptness. Always be on time when you are scheduled to serve.
- Be aware of personal space and don't encroach on someone when you see them squirming.
- Be polite and use your manners. Always.
- You should make an effort to learn someone's name.
- Smile and look your guest in the eye when you shake their hand firmly.
- Don't be too familiar with people, especially with the opposite sex.
- When appropriate (and time allows), introduce yourself and ask their name. If they're rushing to get into the service, that is not the time to strike up a conversation. Be sensitive to their needs.
- Be gentle and friendly when interacting with children. Always be in plain sight and around others when talking with kids.

- Don't point out directions; escort guests to their destination.
- Never embarrass another person.
- Be sensitive to the needs of others.
- Guard against favoritism.
- Be aware of your language. Terms like handicap parking and special needs are appropriate. Don't use the word *invalid* or *disabled*.

Consider Your Appearance

- Modesty is always classy and appropriate.
- Match your congregation. If the majority of your church wears a suit, wear a suit. If the majority of your church dresses casually, dress casually.
- If your team wears a matching T-shirt, wear the T-shirt. If your team wears a lanyard, wear a lanyard. There's no room for rebels on the team.
- Brush your teeth and comb your hair. Keep your hair clean, neat, and free from dandruff. Keep mints in your pockets at all times.
- Trim your beard and mustache.
- Wear deodorant or antiperspirant, but don't overwhelm people with perfume or cologne.
- Wear clean shoes.
- If you're sick or under the weather (running a fever, etc.), ask off and don't expose others to your germs.

CHAPTER 18

SIX KEYS TO SUCCESS

1. BE ON TIME

Please make sure you arrive on time and check in at Team Headquarters. By arriving on time and in your spot, you make sure even the earliest arrivals feel welcome.

2. FOCUS

Stay alert to what is going on at all main doors at all times. Facing those doors at all times will ensure no guest is overlooked. Be especially alert during any music, video, or prayer. During this time, guests will continue to enter, and your presence is crucial in making their entrance comfortable.

3. INTENTIONALITY

Excellence is not random. Everything we do is by design. We create a consistent experience of excellence by functioning inside of a proven set of processes.

4. AUTHENTICITY AND PASSION

The authenticity and passion of our greeting is what people will remember. A greeting that is inauthentic is offensive to our guests. Connecting without passion is forgettable and pointless. Make the most of every opportunity to connect, engage, and honor our guests.

5. TEAMWORK

Nothing great was ever accomplished alone—it takes a team. Our guests are better served when we work together to create the desired warm and welcoming atmosphere of excellence.

6. HAVE FUN!

Having fun is a natural motivator. Anything is easier done when it is made to be fun.

CHAPTER 19

EIGHT TIPS FROM A SECRET SHOPPER

*A*s a secret shopper or mystery worshipper at churches around the country, I've learned a lot about what makes visitors feel welcome. Sometimes I must tell a church I would not return for a second visit, and some of my reasons may be new to you. Whether I'm working with a church plant of 60 people or a megachurch of over 25,000, I always offer the tips below. They're universal and should be present regardless of church size.[16]

Here are eight actions and areas every church needs to address:

1. The Front Door

Before a guest ever steps foot on your church's physical campus, he or she has probably already checked out your church website. What every church should have clearly visible on their homepage is a section or button for first-time guests. Once clicked, this should take the visitor to a page that addresses frequently asked questions (FAQs). These questions may include service times, directions, parking instructions (Is there a side of the building that is better to park on if one has kids?), what to expect (upbeat music and relevant, practical, biblical preaching in a come as you are atmosphere, etc.), what to wear (Are jeans okay? Are shorts okay?), and encouragement for them to be sure to stop by Guest Central

---

16   For more tips, see *Secrets of a Secret Shopper* (Rainer Publishing), by Greg Atkinson.

or your church's Information Booth to pick up a first-time guest packet.

2. What Stinks?

It's important that no church ever underestimates the sense of smell. While sight is the strongest sense for short-term memory, the sense of smell is the strongest and most vivid for long-term memories.

Every church has the potential for positive or negative smells. Mold is a bad smell. Coffee is a good smell. Bleach is a bad smell. Citrus is a good smell. Many churches have restrooms that are disgusting and smell like urine. This lack of attention to detail can be costly and discourage many from ever returning. As best you can, try to walk into the lobby or entrance of your church with a new nose.

3. Park Here

Tim Stevens, when he was executive pastor for a church in Indiana, said every growing church should have someone who is constantly watching its parking. "This is why Visitor Parking is so crucial," he said. "If it's difficult for newcomers to go to your church, they won't go." Some would argue that guests want to remain anonymous and don't want special parking. Of course, some (a minority) want to go unnoticed and will choose to park in regular parking, but for the rest of newcomers, they are appreciative of a close parking space. It's a kind gesture for those willing to try the intimidating and nerve-racking experience of attending a church for the first time. This is especially true for a large church with a huge campus.

4. This Way Parents

One way to assure guests will not return is to have a confusing, long, or hard-to-find process for getting their kids registered and in the right classroom. Wise churches have signage for first-time guest kids' check-in and make the process quick and painless. Regular attendees may know to go up to the check-in kiosk and enter their phone number or swipe their card, but guests will be clueless and need a manned station clearly marked for guests.

Also provide them have a volunteer to walk them through the registration. Then have that person or another helper walk them to their children's classes, explaining what will be going on and how to go about picking their kids up after the service. Signage for the kids' check-in should start in the entryway of the guest parking. Do not assume people know where to go once they enter the building.

5. Give It Away

Something subtle but powerful is a church with a generous spirit. Church of the Highlands in Birmingham, Alabama, is big on this. They have a coffee shop, but they also have a designated area where people can get free coffee. They also give away their message CDs. If you want to bless people and create a generous spirit throughout your church, give away free gifts like these—and other surprises throughout the year. Church of the Highlands hires ice cream trucks to pull up outside the church doors with free treats for everyone leaving on a hot, summer day. What gift could you surprise your guests with this Christmas Eve?

6. Security Counts

One huge issue with visiting families is security. If parents are worried about their child's safety, they will not enjoy the service and will likely not return. A children's classroom must be clean, safe, and secure. Security also includes the check-out process. If anyone can walk into a classroom and pick up a child, you're asking for trouble and will turn off potential newcomers. It's important that your kids' volunteers are trained well and know your church's security procedures for properly connecting parents with their children. This is vital for two reasons: it gives parents peace of mind, and most important, it helps guarantee a tragedy doesn't occur.

7. The Visible Pastor

Accessibility of the senior pastor is another subtle and powerful statement a church can make. Even pastors of the largest churches in America make an intentional and strategic effort to be seen, greeted, and hugged after a service. They may have a bodyguard present for security reasons, but they are available and willing to pray with people who need to speak to their pastor.

Some churches have a designated "Guest Central." Some have a "Meet and Greet" area. Some pastors stand at the front of the auditorium and meet and pray with people. Some walk around the campus shaking hands. Some have an "After Party," with the pastor present and available to meet with newcomers. Especially in a large church, this goes a long way toward countering the rock star or unavailable-pastor preconception many guests bring with them on their first visit.

8. Finish Strong

It's simply not enough for greeters and parking lot attendants to say "Hello" or "Welcome" when one walks into their church. To go to another level, have your first impressions team stationed at their posts when the service ends to say "Goodbye" or "Have a nice week." This goes a long way to wrapping a bow around the entire morning experience and will send visitors off with a lasting positive impression.

Do these eight things and you'll see a greater return and higher percentage of second and third-time guests. Love well. Serve well.

CHAPTER 20

FIVE TIPS TO HELP YOUR TEAM GET READY FOR BIG WEEKENDS

Christmas, Easter, and Mother's Day usually bring larger crowds to church—and greater demands on your Hospitality Team. Here are five practical tips to help your team get ready for the big day. Some of these have been mentioned in other places in this handbook, but each of them is worth repeating, especially when you're challenged to be your best to handle a bigger attendance.

1. Vision cast to your Hospitality/Guest Services Ministry team

So often, people that serve on a church's guest services team feel unimportant. They think they are not good enough to sing on stage, spiritual enough to lead a small group, or tech-savvy enough to serve on the production team. It's vital that your leadership over communicate that Guest Services is not the B-team. This is not a service spot for people who have no talent. This is a vital ministry, a front door to your church. People make up their mind whether or not they will return in the first ten minutes. First Impressions matter!

2. Pray with your team before your first service

Never, ever forget the God factor when you serve in ministry. We are but vessels. We need the Holy Spirit of God to love, lead, and serve through us. Pray each week with your team that they would be the hands and feet of Christ. Pray for God to break down walls of fear, skepticism, and distraction. Pray that the lost would come to Christ and that the hurting would find healing and hope.

3. Remember it's always someone's first Sunday

We really can't stress this enough. No matter the size of your congregation, chances are, someone is entering your doors for the first time. The larger your church, the more this is true. Churches of 200 can expect at least five to eight guests a week. Larger churches welcome even more.

When you gather with your Guest Services team to pray before your first service, remind your team of this simple truth. Focus them on their mission to welcome all who enter with love and to be a servant.

4. Free up your hands

No coffee. No cell phones. The hospitality team should be shaking hands, hugging regular members, holding doors open and pointing to where people need to go (or escorting them there). A team member looking at his cell phone is one of the rudest and worst first impressions you can give a newcomer.

5. Focus on your guests and not your team

It's easy for team members to talk with each other while guests pass by them. Take care to avoid this. Parking lot attendants should be spread out and not bunched up together talking. Door holders, ushers, and greeters should be focused on their role and not engaged in conversation with friends. Make eye contact with all who enter—smile and welcome them.

First impressions matter, so take them seriously and do all you can to remove distractions and barriers for your guests. Love and serve others like you would want to be loved and served.

Finally, give all the glory to God. He is the one who uses us as jars of clay and melts cold hearts. The cool thing is we get to be a part of that supernatural process.

CHAPTER 21

EQUIPMENT AND SUPPLIES

𝓕ollowing are some of the basic supplies and equipment you will want to consider having on hand:

For the Parking Team
  Apparel
  - T-shirts (if your church uses branded shirts for volunteers)
  - Raincoats or ponchos
  - Scarves, hats, hand warmers
  - Supplies
  - Radios (if needed)
  - Safety vests
  - Flashlights/wands
  - Fun things like Mickey Mouse hands and/or greeting signs
  - Cones (if needed)

For Greeters and Guides
  Apparel
  - Church branded shirts (if your church utilizes) and/or lanyards and name badges
  - Supplies
  - Umbrellas and umbrella holders
  - Pop-up tents for gathering outside

- Coolers (ideally on wheels) filled with iced water bottles for volunteers serving outside in the heat

For Welcome Desk Hosts
Apparel
Church branded shirts (if your church utilizes) and/or lanyards and name badges
Supplies
Communication or connection cards and pens

Mints

Tissues

Basic first aid kit

Welcome packet

Gifts for first-time visitors

Information sheets regarding the various ministries and activities of the church

Map of the church building

For Ushers and Section Hosts
Apparel
- Church branded shirts (if your church utilizes) and/or lanyards and name badges

Supplies
- Offering plates/baskets/buckets and envelopes
- Bulletin
- Communication or connection cards and pens
- Mints
- Easy access to water bottles
- Extra Bibles and song books
- Water or a mint
- A Bible

- A pen
- A bulletin or Connection Card

Emergency Supplies
- First-aid kits
- AM/FM radio (with extra batteries)
- Mylar blankets (space blanket)
- Flashlights (with extra batteries)/light sticks
- Whistles (for signaling)
- Garbage/plastic bags (all purpose and for waste disposal)
- Duct tape
- Basic toolkit

CHAPTER 22

FOURTEEN GUEST GIFT IDEAS

*T*hink about what will make guests feel truly noticed and appreciated. Use your creativity (perhaps brainstorm together as a Hospitality Team) and add your own ideas to this list.

1. Branded coffee mug
2. Yeti (or other high-quality) tumbler
3. Small bag of candy
4. Home-baked goods (cookies, pies or cakes)
5. Dinner & a movie (provide microwave popcorn, plus a Redbox gift code, and local pizza restaurant gift card)
6. Gift card (such as, Chick-fil-A, or to a local coffee shop, bookstore, or even a gas card)
7. One-day pass to a nearby amusement park or facility
8. Donation to a local charity in their name
9. Food item from a local bakery (cookies, cupcakes, etc.) or local shop (jar of jam, local honey, etc.)
10. Simple brochure about the church's ministries
11. A trendy gadget of some sort (such as a fidget spinner or a pop socket cell phone grip)
12. High-quality water bottle
13. Moleskine journal or notebook
14. T-shirt (non-cheesy)

CHAPTER 23

IN CASE OF EMERGENCY

*J*t's just a matter of time before you experience some type of emergency situation. When an emergency arises, you must be clear with your instructions and act quickly. It literally can be the difference between life and death.

The information in this chapter is general. Your church should establish and approve its own specific written guidelines for medical emergencies, power failures, fire evacuation, severe weather, and other emergency situations.

Every church should have a medical response team. These team members wear vibrating beepers during the service when they're on duty. They are trained in CPR and defibrillator and supplemental oxygen use.

In General[17]

- Consider training your whole team in first aid and basic lifesaving techniques.
- When an emergency comes up, assign one person to call 911.
- If you have a Medical Response Team, notify them and let them do their job.

---

17   Government websites can be a good source for emergency information. Much of the contents here originated with FEMA (Federal Emergency Management Agency) https://www.fema.gov Another government website that has a wealth of emergency information is: https://www.ready.gov.

- Station someone outside to direct paramedics to the patient's location.
- Have someone stay with the hurt person at all times.
- Pray for the person's recovery.
- Don't allow a crowd to gather around the person.
- If the person in need of help can safely be moved, take them to a private room.
- Relay how they say they're feeling to health care professionals by telephone or when they arrive.

Evacuation Plan

Evacuation plans are for any event where you need to move people outside the facility including: fire, active shooter, bomb threat, earthquake, gas leak, hazardous chemical spill, or floods.

The following are guidelines for creating an evacuation plan for your congregation. Please note that this is not an all-inclusive plan; it is a starting point to developing a specific plan that will meet the needs of your congregation.

The following questions should be answered:

- How would an evacuation plan be activated?
- Are there adequate smoke detectors? Are they checked annually?
- Who would activate an evacuation plan?
- How will first responders be notified? Who will notify first responders?
- Do you have evacuation routes and are they posted?
- Where would people meet after an evacuation? Is there a rally point established?
- Who would be in charge after the evacuation?
- Who would be the spokesperson to first responder personnel (fire, police, paramedics)?

- Do you have a mechanism for accounting for all persons known on site?
- Do you have first aid supplies? Where are they kept?
- Do you have personnel trained in first aid?
- Do you have an inventory of contents?
- Do you have adequate insurance to cover replacement of inventory?
- Do you have adequate relocation insurance?
- Do you have adequate liability insurance?
- Is there a mechanism to review insurance annually?
- Are combustibles stored in fireproof containers or rooms?
- Are combustibles marked appropriately?

All leaders should know the emergency evacuation routes and procedures for the building and their designated assembly area outside the building. Memorize the exit route closest to your work area or office.

The designated assembly areas are located: (provide primary and alternate locations here). Should the designated assembly area be deemed unsafe, an alternate assembly area will be located (provide location here).

If a building evacuation is initiated, remember

- Remain calm.
- Follow the instructions of the incident coordinator or emergency response team, if applicable.
- If you occupy an enclosed classroom or office, close the door as you leave.
- Use stairwells (do not use elevator) for evacuation. Be alert for other staff, members, and emergency agency personnel who might also be using the stairwells.

- Do not return for coats, purses, briefcases, etc., after you have left the area.
- Do not return to your area until the "all clear" signal is given.
- Ensure that a designated person has a plan and procedure to follow in assisting those who may need assistance during an evacuation (such as the elderly, babies, and disabled).
- Emergency Evacuation Procedures should be provided to all members (e.g. in member orientations).
- Once a plan is developed and approved, the plan should be shared with all staff, the congregation, and community partners.
- Do not forget to share your plan with local emergency management officials.
- The plan should also be exercised with drills and simulations at least annually.

Disasters and Other Extreme Situations

Look through the following list, and you'll come to two conclusions: (1) maybe none of these have happened at your church, but (2) you know all of them have happened more than once at other churches. Hospitality Team members can help to facilitate a good response in any of these emergencies:

Fire and Smoke Emergencies

If you detect smoke and/or fire:
- Activate the manual fire alarm.
- Initiate evacuation procedures for any occupants of the affected building(s).

- Call 911 (move to a safe area before making this call).
- Give your name, telephone number, and location.
- Describe the situation.
- If you know how to use a fire extinguisher and feel the best course of action is to attempt to extinguish the fire, locate an extinguisher and, without risking injury, attempt to extinguish the fire.
- If the fire is beyond the point of a safe attempt to extinguish it, isolate the fire by closing doors in the area before evacuating.

Gas Leak

If you think you have a natural gas leak, go to a safe location and call 911 and your natural gas provider. Signs of a natural gas leak include:

- A "rotten egg" odor.
- A blowing or hissing sound.
- Dead or discolored vegetation in an otherwise green area.
- Flames, if leak has ignited.
- Dirt or dust blowing from a hole in the ground.
- Bubbling in wet or flooded areas.

Bomb Threat

All bomb threats should be taken seriously; most threats are received by phone. Act quickly but remain calm.

- Be courteous and listen to the caller.
- Try to keep the caller on the line for as long as possible.
- Get attention of another person and give note, "Call 911! Bomb Threat!"

HOSPITALITY MINISTRY VOLUNTEER HANDBOOK

- If your phone has Caller ID Display, record the incoming phone number.
- Write down the exact words of the caller and threat.
- Don't hang up the phone, leave line open.
- Notify someone in charge.
- Activate the fire alarm to evacuate the building.
- Assist visitors out of the building and proceed to the designated rally zone.
- Remain in the rally zone until "all clear" is issued.

Earthquake

An earthquake is one of nature's most dangerous events because it occurs suddenly with no warning.

Before
- Identify safe places in your building that would offer you protection from falling objects (under desk, table, pew or inside wall).

During
- When shaking starts "Drop, Cover, and Hold On."
- If there is no desk or table, sit on the floor against an interior wall away from windows, bookcases, or other tall objects that could fall on you.

After
- After shaking stops, check yourself and those around you for injuries. Administer first aid to injured victims as needed.
- Conduct a safety inspection of the building for structural damage and hazards.
- If building or work area has sustained significant damage rendering the building unsafe, evacuate the building.

- Assist visitors out of the building to the designated rally zone.
- Don't re-enter the building until it has been deemed safe.

Severe Weather

Know where to evacuate people in case of a flood, tornado, or other severe weather. Have a plan to quickly move everyone to a predetermined safe location to wait out the storm. Have weather radios on hand to keep updated on the storm.

The National Weather Service has developed a method of identifying storm conditions that foster the development of tornadoes.

The classification and definitions of storm conditions are:
- Tornado watch
- Tornado warning
- Other severe weather watch or warning

A tornado watch status indicates that weather conditions are favorable for the development of tornadoes. The tornado watch areas are usually large geographic areas, covering many counties or even states that could be affected by severe weather conditions, including tornadoes. A tornado warning is an alert issued by the National Weather Service after a tornado has been detected by radar or sighted by weather watchers or by the public.

The National Weather Service provides the approximate time of detection, the location of the storm, and the direction of movement. A tornado can move from 25 to 70 miles per hour, so prompt emergency action must be taken.

During a tornado warning, a battery-powered radio should be used and tuned to the National Weather Service and local weather watchers radio frequency. Should a tornado develop which threatens your area, emergency response team members should initiate actions to notify and protect all staff, members, and visitors in the facility.

If a Tornado Warning Is Announced

- Move to a designated tornado shelter area immediately.
- Move quickly, but do not run.
- Do not use elevators.
- Assist disabled personnel in your area.
- Shelter in place until you hear an announcement from a member of the safety response team and/or a hand-held radio system station (if applicable) that it is safe to return to your area.

Tornado Safety Basics

Familiarize yourself with the basics of protecting yourself wherever you may be. If you are indoors, the general responses to a tornado warning are:

- Move away from windows. If you have time, close any window blinds or shades to help prevent flying glass and debris.
- Warn others. Encourage them to get to safety immediately.
- Move away from large expanses of unsupported ceilings.
- Move away from building perimeter area.
- Move to an interior room away from windows—to an enclosed room or conference room, a rest room, an interior stairwell.
- If in an interior hallway, away from windows, crouch down as low as possible.

- If you are in an elevator, stop immediately—get off at the next floor and take cover in an interior hallway or interior room. Do not use elevators during tornado warnings.
- If moving to a safer location in the building is not possible, get under a desk or table in an interior office.
- Once you've situated yourself in the safest place you can find, protect your face and head, and stay where you are until an all clear signal is given.

In general, gymnasiums are not good.

If you are outdoors, the general responses to a tornado warning are:

- If at all possible, move indoors to an interior room.
- If moving indoors is not possible, take cover near objects that are low and securely anchored to the ground, such as culverts or a low retaining wall.
- Remember that outdoor sirens are designed to notify citizens outdoors. Sirens don't have an all-clear signal or sound.

Intruder/Active Shooter Plans

When a hostile person(s) is actively causing deadly harm or the imminent threat of deadly harm or is barricaded within a building, the following procedures should be followed:

- Lock yourself in the room you are in at the time of the threatening activity.
- If communication is available, call 911 or other appropriate emergency numbers.
- Don't stay in open areas.

- Do not sound the fire alarm. A fire alarm would signal the occupants in the rooms to evacuate the building and thus place them in potential harm as they attempted to exit.
- Lock the window and close blinds or curtains.
- Stay away from windows.
- Turn all lights and audio equipment off.
- Try to stay calm and be as quiet as possible.
- If for some reason you are caught in an open area, such as a hallway or auditorium, you must decide what action to take. You can try to hide, but make sure it is a well-hidden space or you may be found as the intruder moves through the building looking for victims.
- Keep any objects you can between you and the hostile person(s) while in the building.
- If you think you can safely make it out of the building by running, then do so. If you decide to run, do not run in a straight line. Use trees, vehicles, or any other object to block you from view as you run.
- When away from the immediate area of danger, summon help any way you can and warn others.
- If the person(s) is causing death or serious physical injury to others and you are unable to run or hide, you may choose to play dead if other victims are around you.
- The last option you have, if caught in an open area, may be to fight back. This is dangerous, but depending on your situation, this could be an option.

- If you are caught by the intruder and are not going to fight back, follow their directions and don't look the intruder in the eyes.
- Once law enforcement arrives, obey all commands. This may involve your being handcuffed or made to put your hands in the air. This is done for safety reasons, and once circumstances are evaluated by law enforcement, they will give you further directions to follow.

Warning Signs

It must be stressed that if you have had contact with *any* individuals who display the following tendencies, you may contact law enforcement, and certainly notify leaders in your organization:

- Threatens harm or talks about killing others.
- Constantly starts or participates in fights/regularly initiates domestic violence.
- Loses temper and self-control easily.
- Swears or uses vulgar language most of the time.
- Possesses or draws artwork that depicts graphic images of death or violence.
- Becomes frustrated easily and converts frustration into uncontrollable physical violence.

Everyday First Aid

Your team needs to be aware of possible first aid problems and have a plan for addressing them. Sooner or later in every congregation, someone will have a heart attack or seizure during weekend worship services, someone will have a cut or a broken bone or a burn on an outing or retreat, or someone will become ill with one of a dozen common problems. We can't pretend this won't happen or be unprepared to help when it does.

Some churches designate a nurse on-call at every service. Smaller churches may know one or two people in the congregation with expertise. You may consider basic first aid training for your hospitality team. One low-cost option for doing this is to contact the Red Cross for a volunteer trainer. You can also search "Basic First Aid Instructions" online to find first aid information and instruction.[18]

---

18 Some examples from the Web (links good at the time of this writing) include:
https:// www.verywellhealth.com/basic-first-aid-procedures
https:// first-aid-product.com/free-first-aid-guide.html; https
https://www.redcross.org/take-a-class/first-aid/performing-first-aid/first-aid-steps

EMERGENCY CONTACTS

911: _____

Medical response team phone numbers:

_____

_____

_____

_____

Fire Department phone number: _____

Police phone number: _____

Poison control phone number: _____

Lead Pastor phone number: _____

Executive or Associate Pastor phone number: _____

Deacons and/or Elders phone numbers:

_____

_____

_____

_____

Team Leader's phone number: _____

Building Manager (if applicable): _____

Electric company: _____

Water company: _____

Gas (if applicable): _____

Telephone company: _____

Other key contacts and their phone numbers:

_____

_____

_____

_____

CHAPTER 24

QUESTIONS FOR
PERSONAL REFLECTION

*C*onsider these questions alone, during your prayer time. Consider praying about a different question here each day. Jot your thoughts under each of these headings.

1. Why am I serving on the Hospitality Team?

2. Do I know, and can I explain my church's core values and mission statement?

3. What one or two things can I do immediately to improve my service on the Hospitality Team?

4. How well do attendees (regulars and guests) see Jesus in me when they come to our church?

5. Am I willing to go the "extra mile" in my service of others?

6. Do I display a positive attitude at all times?

7. Do I maintain pure attitudes and actions toward members of the opposite sex?

8. In the last four Sundays I've served, how many have I been on time, and how many have I arrived late? What can I do to make sure I'm always on time?

9. Which of the following qualities describe my attitude toward serving: Excellence? Humility? Positive? Servant? Teachable?

10. Am I committed to the mission of my church?

11. Who could I recruit to join our Hospitality Team?

12. How could I become more proactive in my service with the Hospitality Team?

CHAPTER 25

DISCUSSION QUESTIONS

*U*se the following questions to prompt discussion at Hospitality Team member meetings. You may want to jot down your answers or insight from other team members in the space provided.

1. Tell about a time you visited an unfamiliar church. How does that experience motivate you to serve well on our Hospitality Team?

2. Tell about a time you experienced great hospitality at a restaurant, hotel, theme park, or some other commercial establishment. How could our church provide a similar experience to guests?

3. How does the Great Commission (Matthew 28:16-20) motivate you to serve in your specific role on the Hospitality Team?

4. What does the Great Commandment (Matthew 22:36-40) mean to us as we serve each week?

5. Name three ways to practically apply the Golden Rule (Matthew 7:12) in your particular area of service.

6. What favorite Scripture passage, verse, or story fuels your desire to serve? Why?

7. If you could choose one way our church could improve its hospitality, what would it be? What it would take to make this improvement happen?

8. Finish this sentence: "The role I play on our Hospitality Team is important, because…"

9. What is one way our church could be friendlier?

10. How can we improve our guest readiness?

11. Role play with your group: Write each of the following situations on a different slip of paper. Put the slips in a basket. Ask a group member to pull out a slip and respond to the prompt written on it. After he or she is finished, the rest of the group can add to the answer:

- A young mother needs to change her child's diaper. How do I help her?

- Someone needs a janitor for a problem in the restroom. What do I do?

- A new guest wants to take her 3-year-old to his class.

- A visitor asks how to become a member of your church. What do I tell them?

- Someone comes to you and asks what denomination your church is affiliated with. What do you tell them?

- Someone asks you how your church is different from the other churches in town. What do you say?

- A guest wants to give an offering, but he didn't get this done during the offering time. How do I help him?

- A newcomer wants to know if you have a women's ministry. Her friend wants to know if you offer something for those with special needs. What do you tell them?

12. Look at each of the case studies sprinkled throughout Section Two. Suppose you are the hospitality volunteer mentioned in each one (parking lot attendant, greeter, etc.). With your group, role play how you would interact with a visitor in a similar situation.

CHAPTER 26

HOSPITALITY HAS AN IMPACT!

*T*alk to other Hospitality Team members, and you're sure to hear testimonies from people whose lives are enriched because of their service.

Here's what a few told us when we asked:

> *When we first came to this church five years ago, we didn't know anyone, and we were overwhelmed with the crowds here. Several members of the hospitality team helped us overcome the barriers and feel comfortable in the new congregation.*
>
> *As a result of that, we joined the hospitality team ourselves! That is our favorite service here . . . to be able to meet visitors, to see that they're sometimes a bit disoriented by the crowd, and to introduce them to the people who will help them get comfortable with the church.*
>
> **— Joe,** insurance agent

> *I appreciate their smiles and learning what makes them tick, saying "Hello, how are you today?" and exchanging greetings.*
>
> **— Ethel,** retired senior citizen

> *The main thing is that you have the role of being the face of the church. You have this role to connect with people so that when they come here, they feel recognized and accepted.*

When they come in, they feel like an outsider, but you can be that person to give them a totally different perspective. "They want me here. They appreciate that I'm here. I don't need to be anxious anymore." When you do that, you literally see a change on their face. That's why I do this. It's just thrilling to see that happen.

— **Andre,** businessman

It's a big job to recruit greeters for all the doors in our building. But I keep working at that week after week, because I know what a difference it makes. Some people are surprised and others open up with big smiles when a friendly greeter meets them at the door. That makes it all worthwhile.

— **Sally,** church administrative assistant

What's Your Testimony?

Why do you serve in your role on the Hospitality Ministry Team? Write down your answer to this question and share it with at least one other person on the team.

CHAPTER 27

CAUGHT IN THE ACT OF SERVING

*U*se this space to record big and little impacts you see from your church's hospitality ministry. Ask God to show you how he's touching lives because you and your team members serve. Write down what you see so (1) you don't forget it and (2) you can share the experiences with other members of your team. Be sure and tell someone else on your team what you're seeing at your next huddle or team training event.

Because _____ did this (_____),

here's what happened:

Because _____ did this (_____),

here's what happened:

CHAPTER 28

RECOMMENDED RESOURCES

Books

Secrets of a Secret Shopper (Rainer Publishing) by Greg Atkinson

The Comeback Effect (Baker Books) by Jason Young and Jonathan Malm

People Are the Mission (Zondervan) by Danny Franks

First Impressions (Group) by Mark Waltz

Becoming a Welcoming Church (B&H Publishing Group) by Thom Rainer

Fusion (Baker) by Nelson Searcy

Unwelcome (Center for Church Communication) by Jonathan Malm

Beyond the First Visit (Baker) by Gary L. McIntosh

The Power of Moments (Simon & Schuster) by Chip and Dan Heath

Be Our Guest (Disney Enterprises) by The Disney Institute

Conferences

The First Impressions Conference (an annual conference for leaders and volunteers), firstimpressionsconference.com

Facebook Group

Weekend Worship and Guest Services https://www.facebook.com/groups/worshipandguestservices

ABOUT THE CONTRIBUTORS

The Writer
Greg Atkinson is the Founder of Worship Impressions and the First Impressions Conference. Greg is an author, leadership coach, consultant, and member of the Forbes Coaching Council. Greg has worked with churches of all stages and sizes, including some of the largest and fastest-growing churches in the country, as well as with businesses, nonprofits, and organizations such as Josh McDowell Ministries.

The General Editor
Mark A. Taylor served in a variety of editorial, marketing, and management roles in a Christian publishing career that spanned more than 40 years, including 14 years as editor and publisher of *Christian Standard* magazine. In retirement, he continues to take on a variety of editing and writing tasks as well as traveling, gardening, teaching, and serving in his local church.

Equipping Children's Ministry Volunteers

Whether you are part of your church's children's ministry, or thinking about serving in children's ministry, the *Children's Ministry Volunteer Handbook* is for you!

Too often, people view children's ministry as a place to drop off the kids so the adults can listen to the sermon, uninterrupted. They fail to see the power and potential of children's ministry.

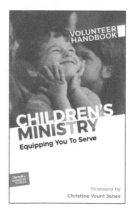

In Matthew 19:13-14, Jesus said, "Let the little children come to me, and do not hinder them, for the kingdom of heaven belongs to such as these." While we may see the naivete of children as a detriment, Jesus sees it as a strength—there is beauty in the simplicity of the gospel. Investing in children's ministry is a worthwhile and crucial part of the church.

This practical handbook features insights from six authors, all experts in the field of children's ministry, with over 100 years of combined experience. They will help guide you through the challenges and joys of children's ministry—and how it is vital to the Kingdom of God.

Be Our Guest

Whether you are a volunteer in your church's guest services ministry, or thinking about serving alongside ushers, greeters, welcome desk hosts, and parking lot attendants at your church, the *Hospitality Ministry Volunteer Handbook* is for you!

How does a member of community see your church? When they hear your church's name, what is their initial reaction? We want any individual who steps foot onto our church campus to immediately feel Christ's love through our actions toward them—the question is, are we doing a good job at accomplishing that mission?

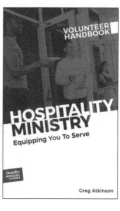

We might not think of customer service and church hospitality in the same vein, but this book shows how a service mentality can make life-changing first impressions on newcomers. It's filled with specific, practical strategies and tools to help the hospitality ministry team show the love of Christ to every visitor.

Join author Greg Atkinson as he helps identify ways your church can increase its hospitality to the community around you, and, ultimately, reach those people for the Kingdom of God.

Practical Outreach Ideas and Ministry Tools

Never has there been a greater need to share the good news of God's love with those in our communities. This compact handbook shows how individual Christians and ministry teams can share the gospel by reaching out to and serving others.

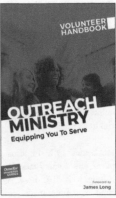

Featuring 121 outreach ideas, this book helps to equip ministry teams with practical tools to serve families, children, youth, seniors, first responders, the oppressed and under resourced, millennials, single parents, local schools and businesses and more!

Designed for ministry volunteers, the book is a compact handbook of outreach ministry helps, which in addition to the dozens of outreach ideas also include outreach Scriptures and prayers, ways to share your faith, team discussion questions and recommended outreach ministries and resources.

This helpful little book is a great resource for equipping outreach ministry volunteers to serve others and to share the good news!

Talk About More Than the Weather

You've driven to the hospital and stand outside a patient's room, ready to knock and ask permission to enter. But then what? How do you make a visit that actually matters?

Here are hundreds of practical tips gleaned from the experience of veteran visitors—chaplains, pastors, and volunteers who've made thousands of visits in hospitals, nursing care facilities, rehab centers, homes, hospice centers, even prisons.

They share what to do, what not to do, and how to connect in caring, compassionate ways with people who may be experiencing the worst days of their lives.

Discover how to make visits that matter—that literally change lives—as you carry the love of Jesus to those who are sick, lonely, or simply curious about the Kingdom.

Biblical Guidance and Practical Advice for Church Elders and Prospective Elders

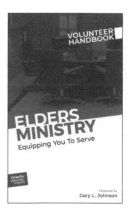

Equip church elders to lead well. More than better methods, the church today needs better leaders. But too often we recruit these leaders (the New Testament calls them *elders*) without equipping them for their vital task. This practical handbook presents the need, lifts up the Bible's vision for elder ministry, and provides a wealth of practical how-to training to help elders provide the spiritual leadership that can't come from anyone else. Elder teams will build unity and confidence as they discuss it together.

Written by the ministry founders and leaders of e2: effective elders, content is based on decades of local-church experience and interaction with everyday elders in hundreds of congregations.

Equip Small Group Leaders to Lead Well

Your church's small group ministry is where faith can get real. Where masks can slide off and honest struggles and doubts surface.

Maybe. It all depends on the leaders of your groups.

Give your leaders the training they need to take group members deeper. To create group cultures that encourage transparency. To cope with questions, deal with doubts, and make disciples.

This book offers your team a lifetime of easy-to-read, easy-to-remember advice from experienced small group ministry leaders.
They share what they've learned, what they wish they'd known earlier, and dozens of proven practical tips that will aid in developing healthy small groups in your church.

A men's ministry that guys will look forward to being a part of!

Every church wants to actively engage and grow men—but most men's ministries have a hard time getting guys in the door. This wildly practical ministry handbook equips men's ministry volunteers and their leaders with proven suggestions for building a program that's magnetic to men.

Give your ministry team the tools, tips, and training they need to help develop the trust and accountability between men which leads to deep, lasting spiritual growth.

Included within this helpful men's ministry guide:

- Practical ways to get men into the Word
- Guidance for effective men's group meetings
- Dozens of ideas for serving together, fostering accountability, strengthening family connections, and more!

Take your Senior Adult Ministry to the Next Level

That's what will happen when you train and equip your Senior Adult Ministry volunteers not just to minister to seniors, but also to minister *with* them. Help deepen seniors' faith and grow their friendships with one another, your team, and with God.

If your church is like most, seniors are mostly on the sidelines, but not by choice! They're hungry for purpose and fellowship. But unless you're actively creating opportunities for connection and contribution, many senior adults feel unneeded and unwelcome and simply drop out.

In this Outreach Ministry Guide you'll discover:
- Dozens of senior-friendly programming ideas
- Guidance and biblical wisdom for helping seniors cope with change, loneliness, and grief
- Ideas for energizing senior adult Sunday school classes, senior-sized service projects, and more!